ARIZONA

THE BEAUTY OF IT ALL

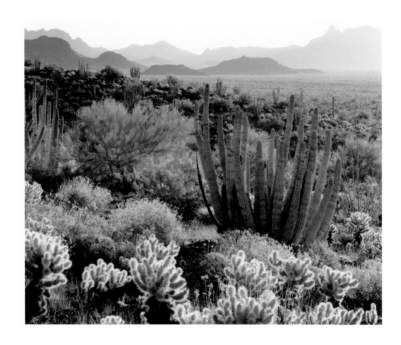

TEXT BY SAM NEGRI   PHOTOGRAPHS BY *ARIZONA HIGHWAYS* CONTRIBUTORS

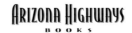

ARIZONA HIGHWAYS
BOOKS

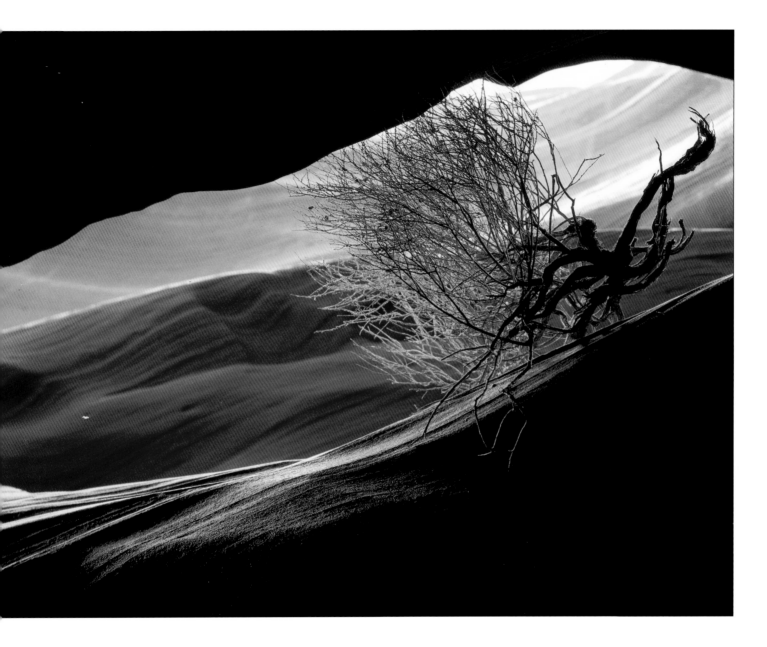

(PREVIOUS PAGE) The sun gilds an array of desert plants at Organ Pipe Cactus National Monument. JACK DYKINGA

(ABOVE) A dried shrub lies where the wind swept it, on a slot canyon's sandstone lip near Page. Fragile products of eons of erosion, slot canyons often seem to be mere fissures in the ground. MICHAEL FATALI

CONTENTS

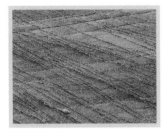
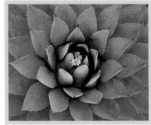
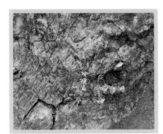
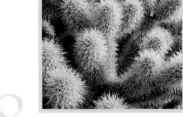
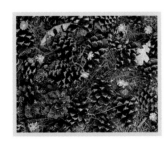
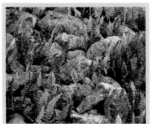
3

BOOK EDITOR: BOB ALBANO   DESIGN: MARY WINKELMAN VELGOS   PHOTOGRAPHY EDITOR: SCOTT CONDRAY   COPY EDITOR: EVELYN HOWELL

Published by the Book Division of *Arizona Highways* magazine, a monthly publication of the Arizona Department of Transportation, 2039 West Lewis Avenue, Phoenix, Arizona 85009.
Telephone: (602) 712-2200   Web site: www.arizonahighways.com

PUBLISHER: WIN HOLDEN   EDITOR: ROBERT STIEVE   SENIOR EDITOR/BOOKS: RANDY SUMMERLIN   ART DIRECTOR: BARBARA DENNEY
PHOTOGRAPHY DIRECTOR: PETER ENSENBERGER   PRODUCTION DIRECTOR: MICHAEL BIANCHI   PRODUCTION COORDINATOR: ANNETTE PHARES

ISBN-13: 978-1-932082-73-9
ISBN-10: 1-932082-73-5

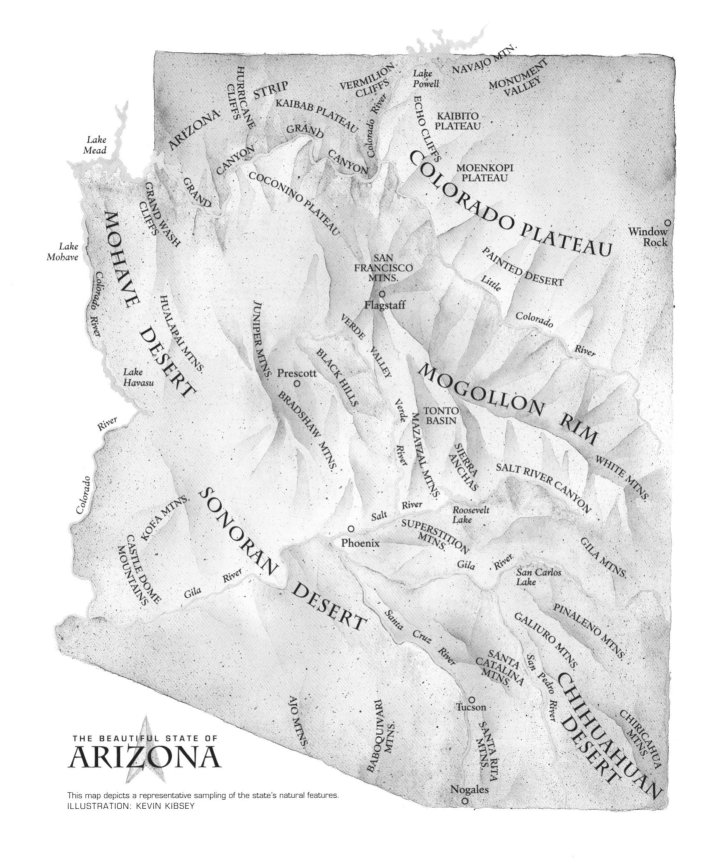

4

PROLOGUE

THORNY PLANTS TYPICAL OF THE CHIHUAHUAN DESERT DOMINATE THE

uplands flanking the San Pedro River in southeastern Arizona. Dry and scrubby, the landscape east of the Huachuca Mountains is speckled with vegetation such as tarbush, creosote, and acacia. A few head of cattle graze on sparse grass. Overhead, vultures and hawks soar on the wind, searching for their dinner.

This scene hardly invites artists to set up easels or photographers their tripods. Why then introduce a book titled *Arizona: The Beauty of It All* with such a description? To find the answer, let's ascend the Huachuca Mountains flanking the valley: even drabness takes on picturesque dimensions when it's viewed from an aerie. On the way, we'll witness the variety underlying the beauty of a state with six — some say seven — biotic divisions based on elevation and called life zones.

On the western edge of the valley floor, the Huachucas rise about a mile, topping out at 9,466 feet on Miller Peak. Deeply creasing this range are forested canyons such as Ramsey, Carr, and Miller, home to hummingbirds, butterflies, and shy woodland life.

From atop the Huachucas, you can see much of southeastern Arizona. The San Pedro Valley and immense landforms beyond it brim with beauty. A verdant ribbon of cottonwoods, willows, and ferns edges the San Pedro River. Hues and shadows dance from tone to tone as the sun and clouds amble overhead.

Getting to this vista takes the explorer through tall grasses, oak, manzanita with its burnt-red bark, juniper, pine, and, finally, aspen. It's from this elevation that the perspective of flatland drabness takes on an unexpected beauty.

And so it goes across the state.

With *Arizona: The Beauty of It All,* the editors of *Arizona Highways* have assembled a description highlighting the state's natural, historical, and cultural heritage, and a medley of images taken by some of America's best landscape photographers. We hope you savor the essence of Arizona's beauty: four deserts and their sprinkling of oases, forested and desert mountains, plateaus marked by monolithic formations, the western regions defined by the lower Colorado River and relatively low ranges, and the Arizona Strip with its 11,000 square miles of desolate plains, deep forests, and arid plateaus.

— *Bob Albano*

(FOLLOWING PANEL, PAGES 6 AND 7) Eerie light after a winter storm casts a surreal glow across bare mesquite trees near Madera Canyon in the Santa Rita foothills. Midway between Tucson and the Mexican border. The canyon is a popular destination known for its colorful birds and other wildlife.
RANDY A. PRENTICE

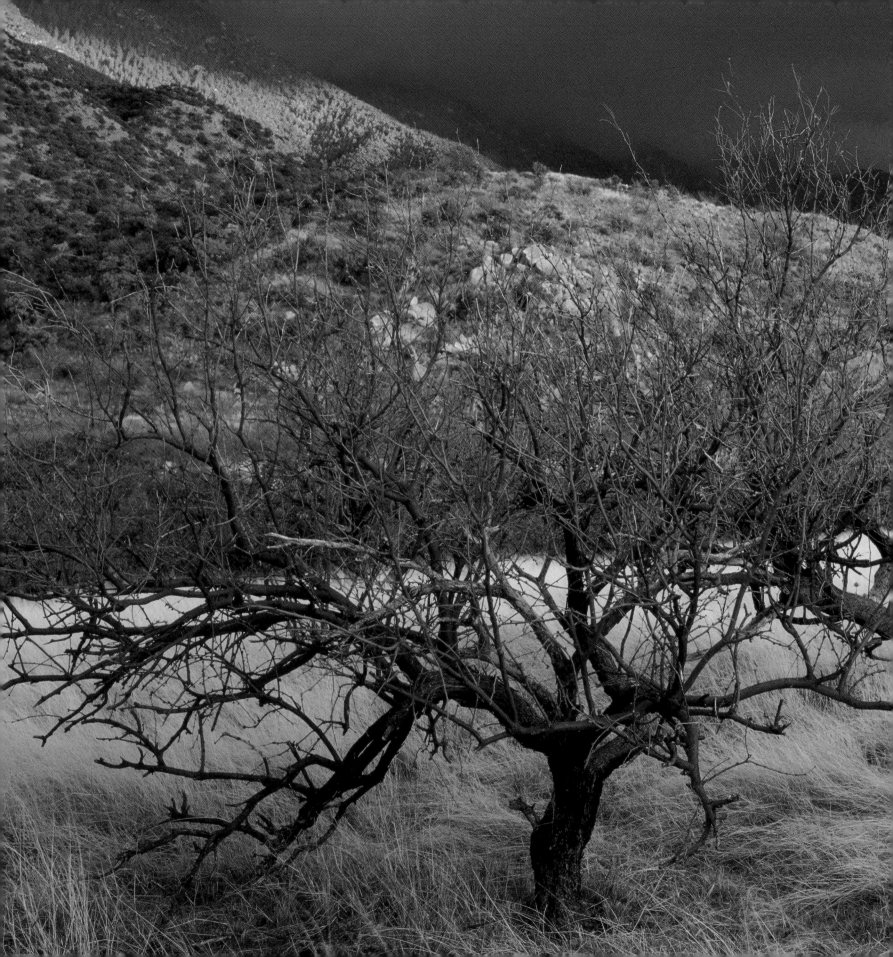

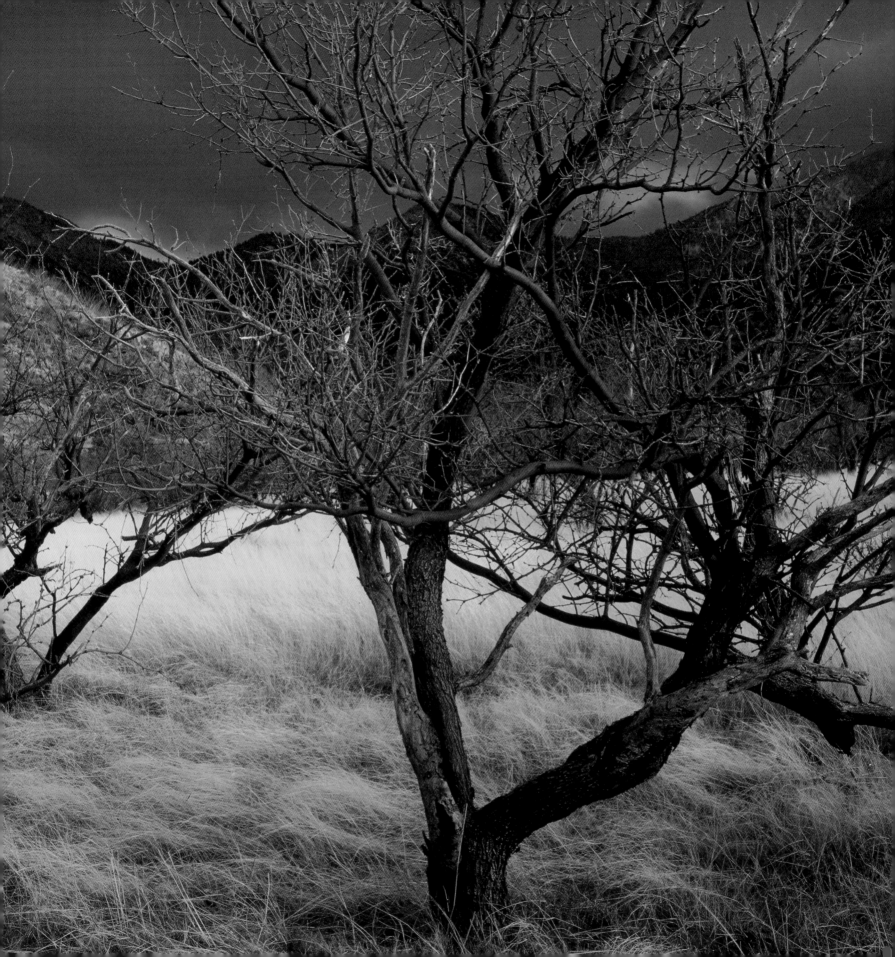

ARIZONA STRIP

THE AREA KNOWN AS THE ARIZONA STRIP — ESSENTIALLY ALL OF

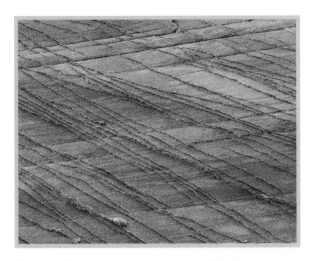

Fracture lines intersecting cross-bedded sandstone layers create a crosshatch pattern in the Paria Canyon-Vermilion Cliffs Wilderness. GARY LADD

northwestern Arizona — is defined by the Colorado River, which flows into Arizona from the north. At the Utah-Arizona border near Page, the Colorado makes a large curve to the south and east, pushing its way between the red bluffs of the Kaibab and Kaibito Plateaus until it reaches Marble Canyon, 128 miles north of Flagstaff. At that point the river says good-bye to the sandstone walls of the Vermilion Cliffs and sharply turns west. For the next 220 miles the Colorado River, second longest river in the United States, careens through its most famous feature, the mile-deep rift called the Grand Canyon.

Once the river turns west, all of the land between the Grand Canyon's North Rim and the Utah border, a giant rectangle on the map, becomes the Arizona Strip, a landscape of desolate plains, deep forests of pine, spruce, and aspen, and arid plateaus covering roughly 11,000 square miles. Split from the rest of the state by the Grand Canyon, this landscape of splendid isolation, as it was once described, consists of about five million acres and three small communities with a combined population of less than 4,500. In this country, everyone has elbow room.

In a landscape where paradox can be found in almost every direction, the Grand Canyon is the greatest paradox of all, a testament to the power of water in a region where water is rare. Scarce as it is, it was water that formed the canyon's sedimentary rocks under ancient seas, and water that carved its buttes and mesas into temples and towers and domes and cathedral-like caves.

Years ago when I camped on an isolated bluff on the North Rim, I thought about John Wesley Powell and his gamble with water. Powell had lost an arm in the Civil War and then went on, in 1869, to explore and map the

Grand Canyon by boat. The physical demands of such an expedition were Herculean, but I was equally impressed by Powell's confidence in his assumptions about water. Before launching his expedition, he'd been warned about the danger of high waterfalls, but Powell was convinced these warnings were unfounded. A river as muddy as the Colorado, he reasoned in the days before the Colorado was dammed, already would have smoothed down any major falls, leaving only rapids to contend with. Powell staked his life on his assumptions, and even if the rapids may have turned out to be more ferocious than he bargained for, his assumptions about the river and waterfalls were basically correct. I liked thinking about Powell as a fanatical gambler who knew what he was talking about.

More than 200 million years ago the land that Powell eventually mapped was covered by an inland sea and swampland that was home to dinosaurs that roamed Arizona's northern tier from Kingman east to the Four Corners. Geologists say that, about 170 million years ago, these seas dried up, leaving great deposits of sand and limestone.

The Arizona Strip began to take the shape it has today some 30 million years ago when a massive block of the earth's crust was uplifted and tilted to the northeast. Over time, volcanic eruptions and erosion divided this huge slab into a series of elongated and nearly isolated north-south trending plateaus — including the Shivwits Plateau (the western-most plateau), the Uinkaret Plateau, the Kaibab Plateau, and the Marble Platform. The cliffs along these plateaus range from 200 to more than 400 feet high.

The Arizona Strip has never been easy to explore. Some idea of its remoteness can be seen in the fact that the Grand Canyon's more accessible South Rim was first seen by Spanish explorers in 1540 when they were led there by Hopi guides, but it was 236 years later before other Spaniards, led by Fathers Francisco A. Dominguez and Francisco Silvestre Velez de Escalante, wandered near the North Rim and crossed a portion of the Arizona Strip. The friars were trying to find an inland route from Santa Fe, New Mexico, to the new Spanish colonies near what now is San Francisco, but hostile Indians and rough terrain forced them northward through western Colorado and central Utah, and they eventually turned back.

On their return, they dipped southward into the Virgin River Valley in the northwestern corner of the Arizona Strip. With winter approaching and food supplies dwindling, they headed south across the Strip, not realizing that the chasm of the Grand Canyon would soon bar their way. A friendly group of Paiutes in effect saved their lives by warning them that their route was impassable and directing them to travel eastward across the Strip to the only possible point to cross the river. That spot on the Colorado River later was named Lees Ferry.

However, even at that point the water was too deep and swift for a safe crossing, so the Domiguez-Escalante party headed up Paria Canyon and traveled north and eastward until they came to a ford in the vicinity of what is now Lake Powell. Today that ford is known as the Crossing of the Fathers.

The Spaniards failed to reach their original goal, yet their achievement was significant: as Dorothy A. House wrote in the Museum of Northern Arizona's *Plateau* magazine, "They were the first white men to traverse the Arizona Strip, the first to identify its principal features, and the first to map it and leave a written record of what they saw."

The next major exploration of northwestern Arizona was done in 1858 by Mormon missionaries. Guided by a Paiute Indian, they left southwestern Utah and

journeyed across the Strip, hoping to encounter and convert Hopis in the pueblos on Second Mesa. They also were looking for new territory to settle.

Later, the route followed by these first Mormons developed into the Honeymoon Trail, so-called because it was used by Mormon couples who traveled from Arizona to have their marriages sanctified at the temple in St. George, Utah. Afterward, they would follow a wagon route south and eastward through the Arizona Strip to Lees Ferry, and eventually into the White Mountains and the Gila River Valley of central Arizona, where their descendants still live.

Certainly there have been some changes in that lonely terrain since those days, but the area remains remarkably primitive. There are an estimated 6,000 miles of dirt roads in the Arizona Strip, but hardly any people. Roughly 1,300 live in tiny Fredonia, 30 miles northwest of Jacob Lake, and there are park rangers at Pipe Spring National Monument, 14 miles west of Fredonia on

State Route 389. At Colorado City, which with some 3,000 residents is the largest community in the Strip, there is a growing religious community of polygamous families, ignored by federal and state officials in recent years.

Perhaps because of its proximity to Utah and perhaps because it is so isolated, the Arizona Strip has for at least 100 years been associated with polygamy. At the end of the 1800s polygamy was outlawed by the federal government, and then by the Mormon church. However, some Mormons who disagreed with the ban, or who couldn't abide by it for practical reasons, simply moved their "extra" wives to Fredonia or Pipe Spring, an area removed from the eyes of prying officials. In 1888 there were so many of these extra wives living at Pipe Spring that the place was jokingly referred to as "Adamless Eden." The families at Short Creek, now called Colorado City, disagreed with the ban on religious grounds and split from the Church of Jesus Christ of Latter-day Saints (the Mormons) and continue the practice of plural marriages to this day.

As the crow flies, Colorado City is only about 40 miles east of an enigmatic spot called Little Black Mountain. Long before polygamists or any Europeans set foot in North America, the ancestors of the Anasazi and more recent Pueblo Indians had left their mark at this lonely mesa just three-tenths of a mile south of the Arizona border.

From my vantage point at Little Black Mountain, I could see only the storm clouds, the wild grasses of the Arizona Strip, and other mountains. But, in the jumble of sandstone boulders all around me, I could also see some 500 pictures of bighorn sheep, snakes, spirals, human stick figures, bear paws, lizards, turtles, and strange designs that could mean anything. The only thing experts will say with any certainty is that these pictures were made over a period of approximately 5,000 years by Indians from different cultural groups.

Where did these people come from? Where did they go? Why did they come to this broken hill that belongs to the sky? My thoughts were swimming in a place without water, 500 miles, it seemed, from the nearest answer. The experts, it turned out, did not know the answers to these questions.

The day I went to Little Black Mountain, I had actually started out for Toroweap. I had crossed the Colorado River at Marble Canyon, where it was raining heavily, and began the rapid ascent from House Rock Valley to Jacob Lake. But three miles below Jacob Lake (named after Mormon leader Jacob Hamblin) the rain turned into a sheet of heavy snow. In a matter of minutes, it seemed, I had gone from 6,000 to 8,000 feet, and the road through the tall pines of the Kaibab Plateau was thick with snow and ice. The Kaibab, the highest of the plateaus extending northward from the Grand Canyon, rises to 9,200 feet. Toroweap, southeast of the Shivwits Plateau, was lower, but getting to the rim would require driving through 45 miles of slick mud, and I had been warned by a stern deputy from the Mohave County Sheriff's Department not to try it.

I had made the trip several years earlier in dry weather and remembered the signs of humans who had given up and gone away — the rusted skeletons of plows and backhoes and the bleached bones of coyotes and the cattle they may have been stalking. I didn't need much persuading to stay away from 45 miles of white-knuckle travel.

This isolated and sometimes perilous land in northwestern Arizona remains a startling world: part forest, part barren and desolate badlands, a graveyard for giant rocks, and sharp red cliffs that lie in the distance. The sky is omnipresent, and every flat-topped mesa or jagged cliff, no matter how close, seems distant and mirage-like.

Ultimately, it is the sky that makes a place like Little Black Mountain Petroglyph Site, with its strange and ancient symbols, seem perfectly reasonable. In this landscape, it is easy to get the feeling that humans are a minor piece of the puzzle.

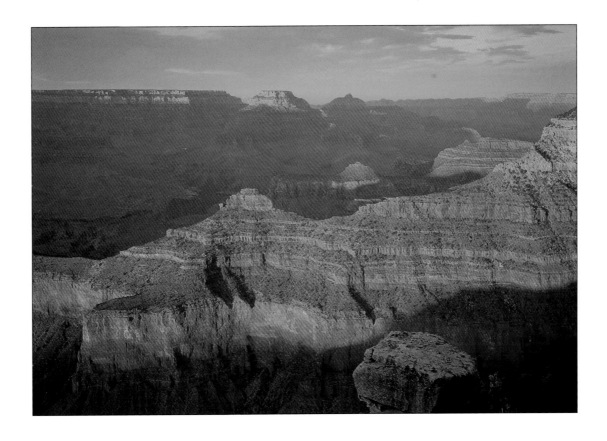

Whether viewed from the South Rim or the North Rim, sunset nearly always heightens the colors of the Grand Canyon.
(ABOVE) O'Neill Butte, shown from Mather Point on the South Rim, was named after Spanish-American War Roughrider William Owen "Buckey" O'Neill. GARY LADD

(RIGHT) Sunset lights a passing rainstorm below Cape Royal on the North Rim. JACK DYKINGA
(FOLLOWING PANEL, PAGES 14 AND 15) Eastern Grand Canyon is viewed from Yavapai Point on the South Rim. DICK DIETRICH

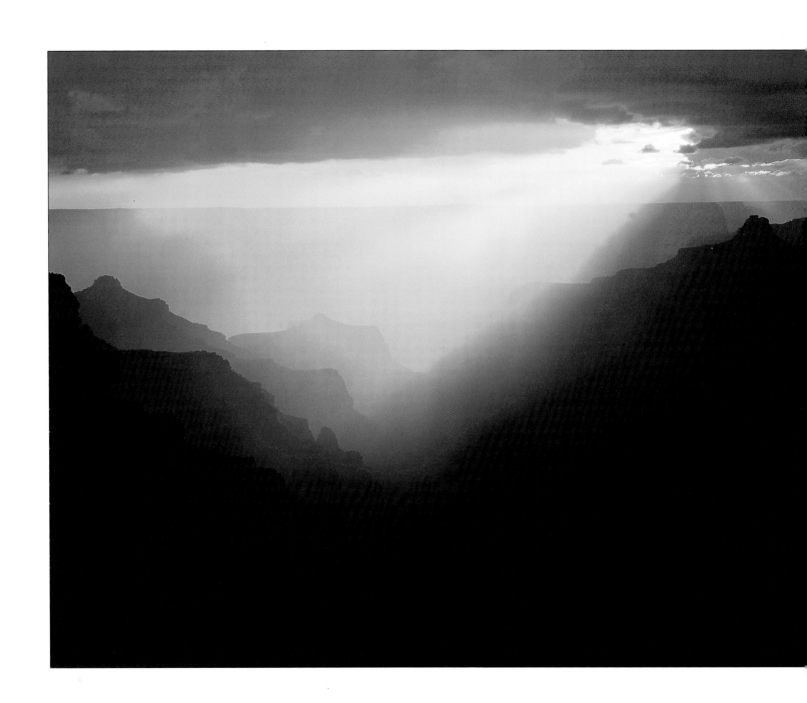

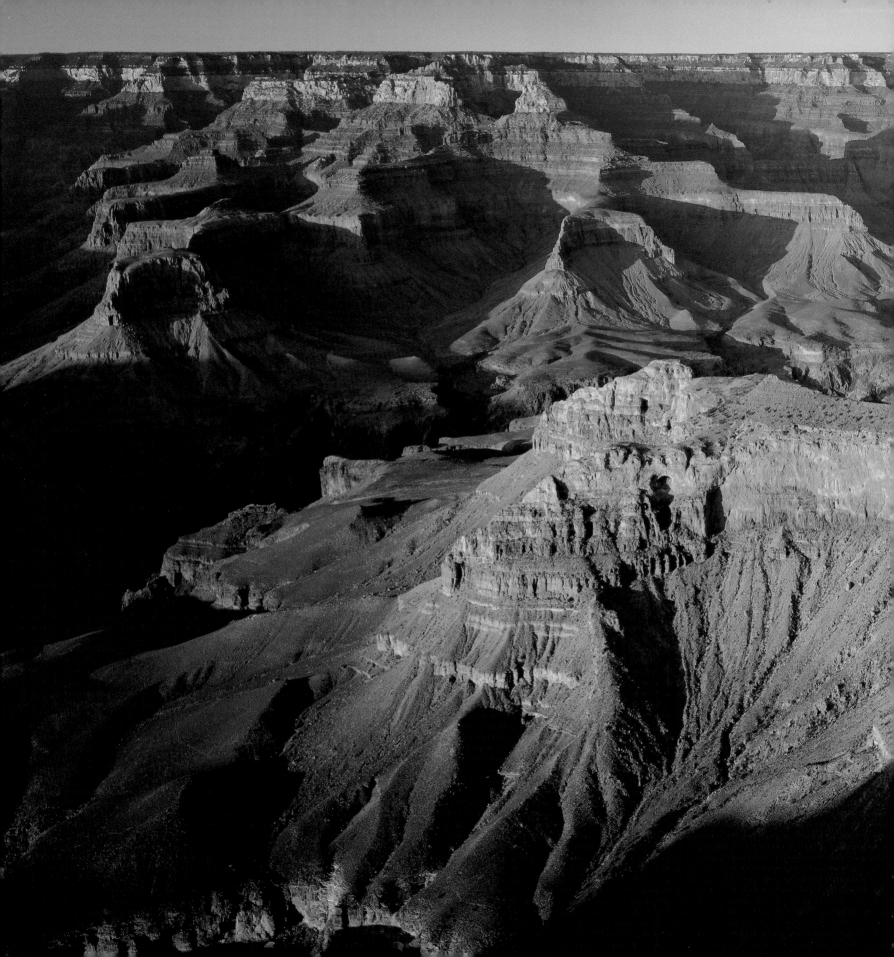

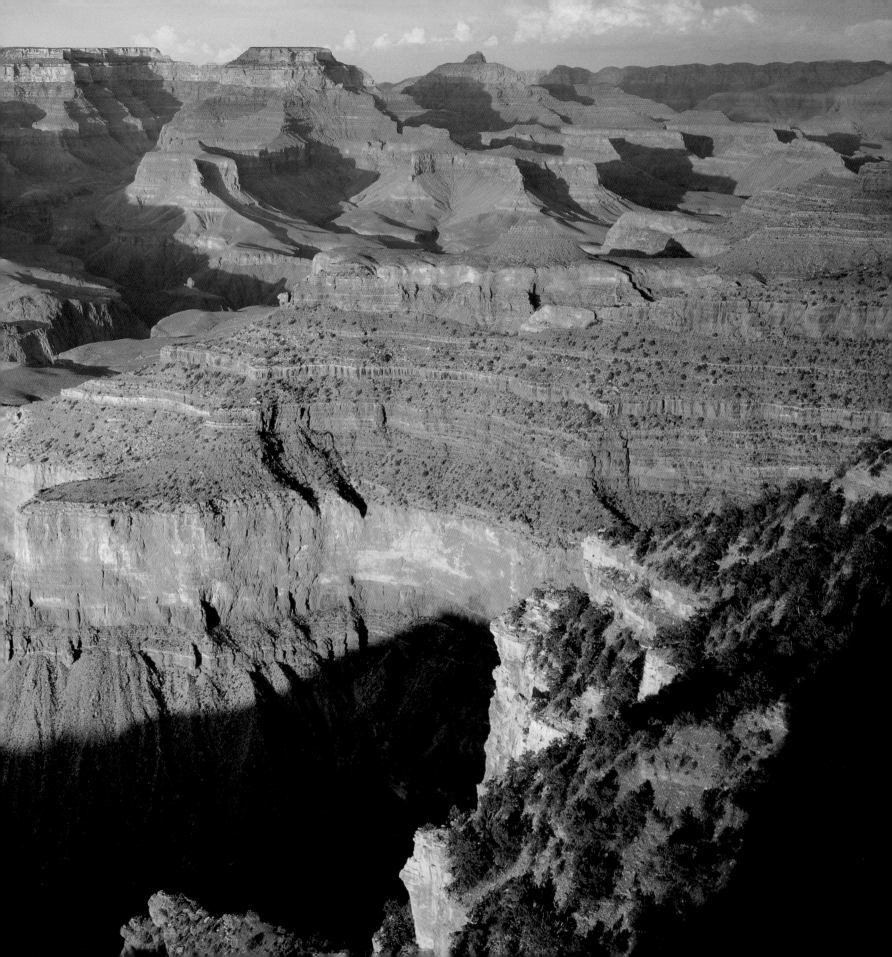

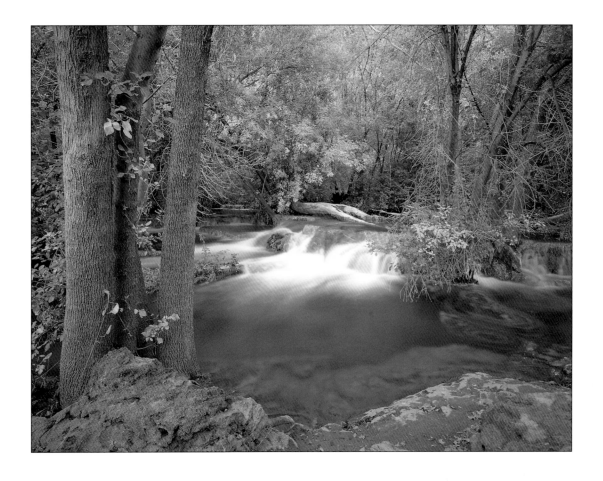

Havasu means "blue water" in the language of the Havasupai Indians. The "people of the blue water" for centuries have lived in their Shangri-la village above the spectacular waterfalls of Havasu Creek at the bottom of the Grand Canyon. (ABOVE) Havasu Creek flows through travertine (calcium carbonate) deposits, which give the water its distinctive color. JERRY SIEVE

(RIGHT) Calcium carbonate left behind by evaporating water creates hanging curtains of stone on the rocks of Mooney Falls. CHARLES CHANLEY

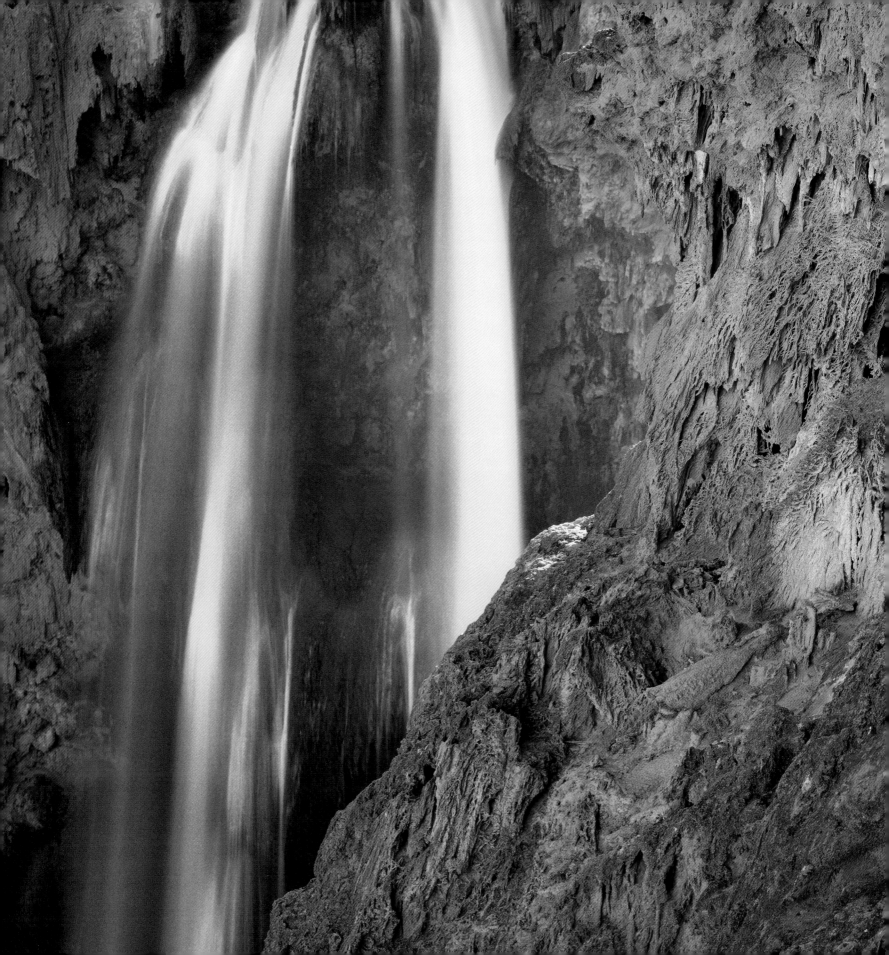

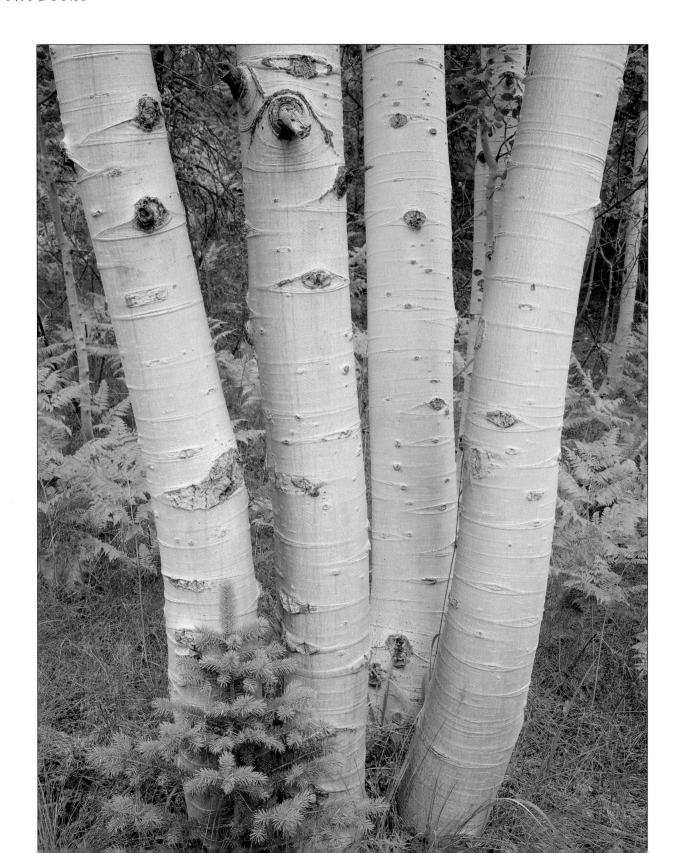

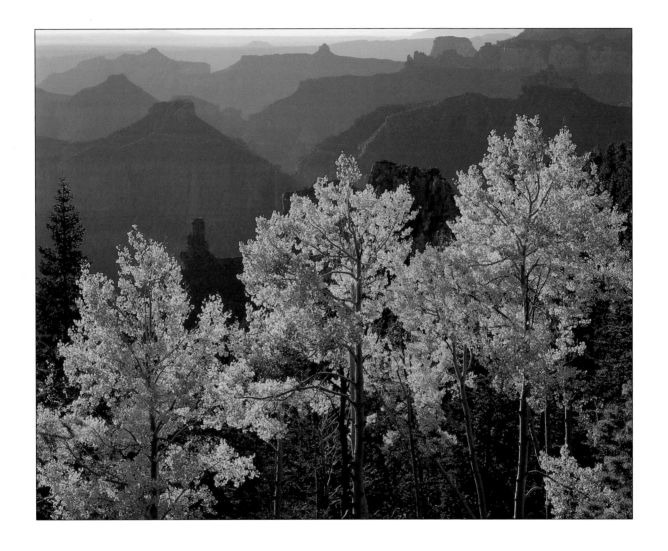

Groves of aspen trees brighten the deep forests of the Grand Canyon's North Rim, their trunks shining ghostly white, their leaves softly shimmering pale green in summer and brilliant gold in autumn.

(LEFT) A quartet of aspen boles shelters a young spruce. JEFF GNASS
(ABOVE) Sunset illuminates autumn aspens. MICHAEL FATALI

(FOLLOWING PANEL, PAGES 20 AND 21) Wind and water erode delicate swirls into the soft sandstone of the Paria Plateau. MICHAEL FATALI

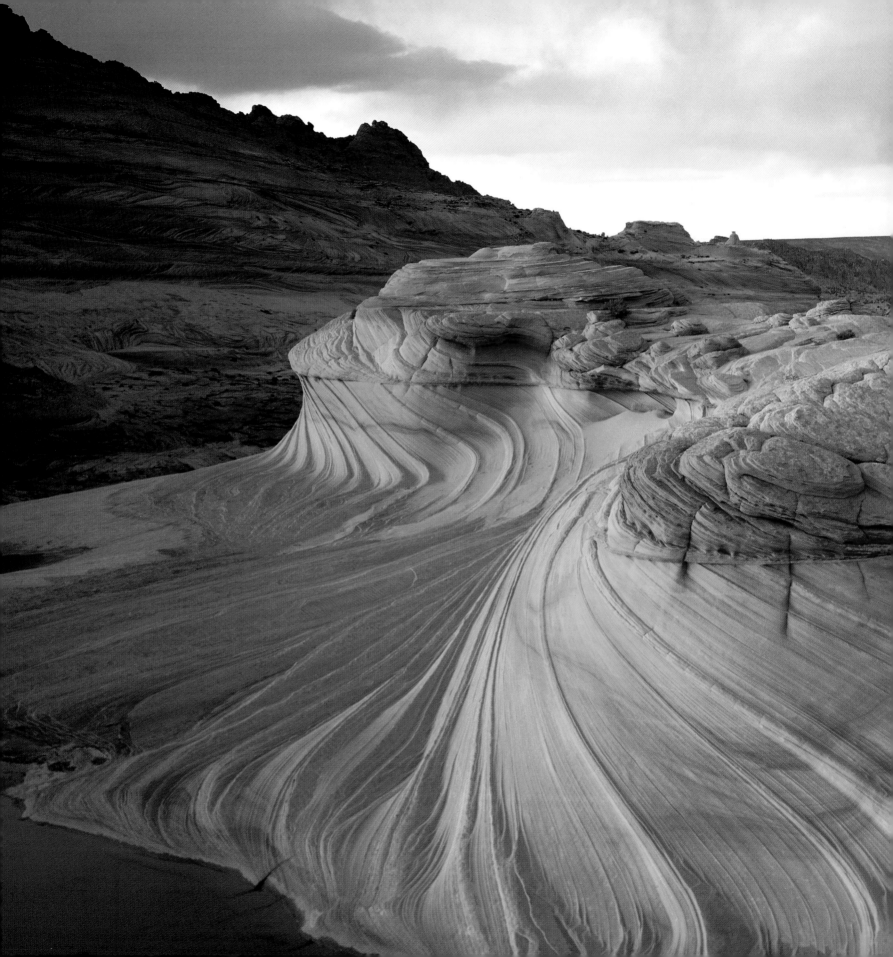

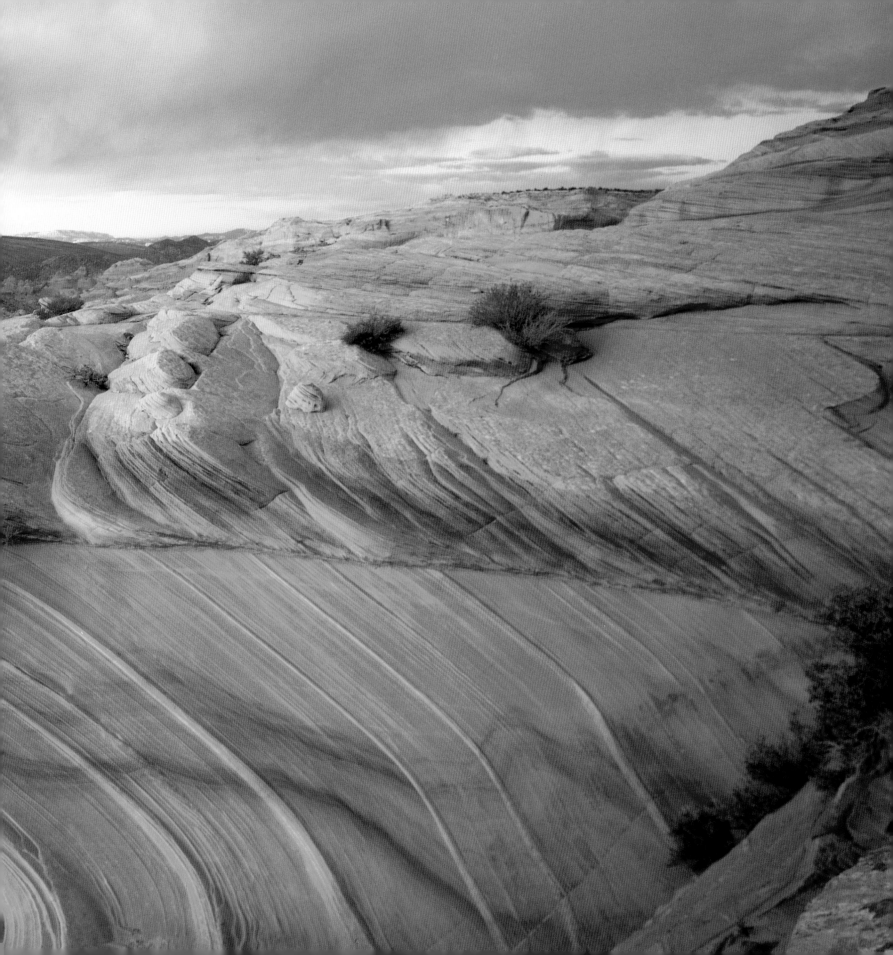

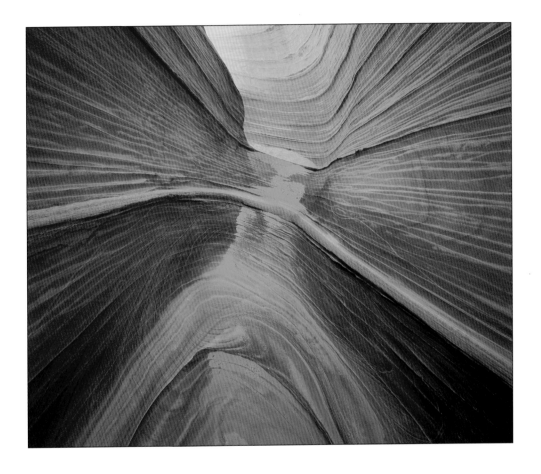

Ages ago, an inland sea covered what is now northern Arizona and compressed layers of sand into stone. Iron deposits in the sand oxidized, coloring the stone in hues ranging from beige to pale pink to vermilion.

Erosion sculpted the sandstone into the fantasy textures and shapes found in the area today.

(ABOVE) Racing water cutting through this arroyo exposed the layering of sandstone in the Vermilion Cliffs. STEVE BRUNO (RIGHT) A rain pool reflects sandstone sculptures near Lake Powell. MICHAEL FATALI

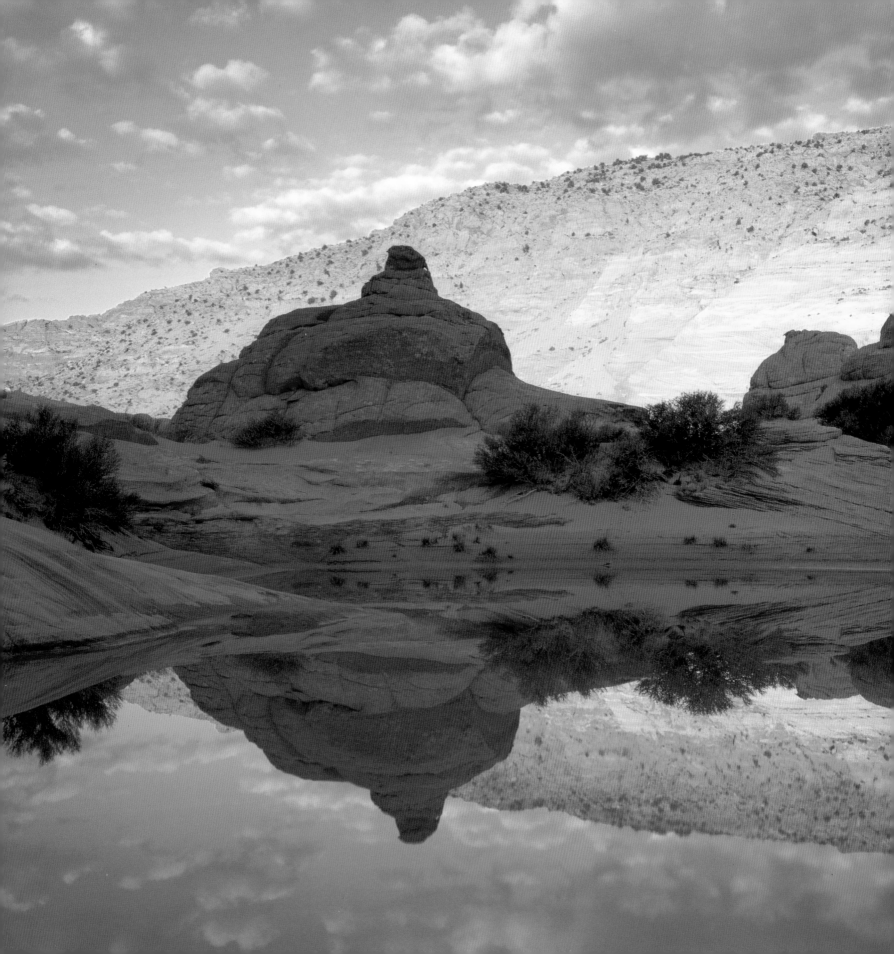

INDIAN COUNTRY

JUNIPER LOGS ARE EASY TO SPLIT. WHACK A JUNIPER LOG WITH A SMALL

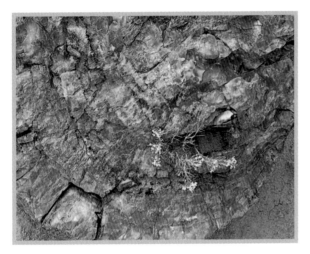

Western peppergrass sprouts from a stone log in the Jasper Forest at Petrified Forest National Park.
JACK DYKINGA

ax and the fresh wood displays the dominant color of the northeastern third of Arizona. For several days I had been searching for a color that would remind me of the buttes and mesas of Monument Valley, Canyon de Chelly, and Tsegi Canyon, where the Anasazi cliff dwellings of Betatakin and Keet Seel lie hidden. Then I went home and split some juniper and saw the burnt red, not quite cherry, not quite mahogany, something like wine or maroon but neither of those. The split wood provided not only the color, but also the fragrance. It is the fragrance of fresh air that evokes long stretches of unpopulated red hills covered with fine sands, sage, and chaparral. It is the color of the landscape the Hopi and Navajo Indians call home.

Just as an acorn is inextricably part of the cycle that will produce an oak tree, so the Hopis and Navajos are intimately part of the landscape that nourished their ancestors. A number of these people will leave their native habitat and move to the cities to find work, and some will become part of a world where track lighting and vertical blinds are highly regarded, but sooner or later many will return to the hogan or kiva for the comfort that only continuity can provide.

As James E. Cook wrote nearly 30 years ago for the *Arizona Republic* newspaper: "Reservations have become more important than tracts of land on which the invaders placed Indians until they could decide what to do about them. A Native American may have two degrees, a position with the firm, a working wife and belong to Toastmasters. When Anglo craziness gets to him, he returns to the reservations to sort it out. This is a more spiritual experience than a white Arizonan's return to the ancestral home in Iowa."

This homeland, the Colorado Plateau, is a landscape of swirling sandstone cliffs, narrow canyons, and orange walls where time and geologic collision have created a rich canvas. The region's distinctive cliffs and pinnacles — the long mesas and squat buttes carved by wind and waterborne silt — cover 150,000 square miles in northern Arizona and New Mexico, western Colorado, and eastern Utah. Various iron compounds and other minerals aged in these cathedral-like formations and, over a billion years or so, produced the red, brown, black, and maroon tapestry visible today in the walls and outcroppings of the Grand Canyon, Monument Valley, Canyon de Chelly, the Painted Desert, and the Petrified Forest.

Long before I knew anything whatsoever about the religious beliefs of Hopis and Navajos, I concluded that anyone born and raised near the dramatic sandstone buttes and mesas of Monument Valley or Canyon de Chelly, to name just two remarkable locations, probably had a sense of the world significantly different from anyone growing up in a major city. If nothing else, the Indians of the Colorado Plateau have had the luxury of living in a world that was largely silent except for the sound of tunneling wind or the long cries of coyotes passing in the dark.

That the land is beautiful and evocative of a less populated America is obvious. Less obvious is the fact that it's a tough place to survive, not only because of the scarcity of jobs, but because of the arid conditions. Indians raise corn, beans, squash, sheep, and cattle in this country, but not easily. The plateau province is high desert, attracting roughly eight to12 inches of rainfall a year, and the growing season is a relatively short 133 days. Both traditional Hopis and Navajos rely, to some extent, on supernatural forces and complicated rituals to moderate the harshness of these conditions.

The Hopis, cultural descendants of the Ancestral Puebloan cliff dwellers, do this with their kachina dances, when men dress up in elaborate costumes and masks. Kachinas — there are roughly 400 of them in the Hopi pantheon — are invisible spirits representing, as the expert Barton Wright put it, "the spirit essence of everything in the real world." The real world of the Hopis includes 11 villages perched on the rocky spurs of northeastern Arizona's Black Mesa, a diamond-shaped plateau some 2,200 feet above the surrounding country, as well as newer settlements at the bases of First Mesa and Third Mesa. Among the mesa-top villages is Oraibi, founded around A.D. 1150 and said to be (along with Ácoma Pueblo in New Mexico) the oldest continuously inhabited town in the United States.

Through their elaborate kachina dances and ceremonies that begin in November or December and continue until late July, the Hopi believe they create a balance between the visible world and the spirit world. The kachina dances may bring moisture to the land, nourishment from crops, obedience to children, and a general sense of happiness and well-being to the community. When any of these elements are out of balance, the kachina ceremonies are believed to restore harmony. Hopis believe the prayers of their spiritual elders hold the land in the entire western hemisphere in balance for all living creatures, including humans.

The Navajos, who settled on the plateau after the Hopis, migrated to the Southwest from western Canada around 1,000 years ago. Like the Hopis and other pueblo peoples, the Navajos believe everything has a spiritual as well as a material side, but where the Hopis achieve healing and balance through their kachina ceremonies, the Navajos resort to complex ceremonials conducted by trained medicine men called singers. Every important act in the Navajo ritual is accompanied by a specific chant.

As the anthropologist Leland Wyman observed, "A singer specializes in one or two (or at most half a dozen) complete chants because each one is a vast complex of songs, prayers, ritual acts, plant medicines, material properties, and symbols." The chants, which may last from two to nine nights, are said to be effective in curing everything from a witchcraft curse to insanity.

All of these exotic rituals are performed in a landscape that is spiritually significant to the Indians who inhabit it. The Navajos, for example, believe that when their gods rose to the earth's surface from the underworld, they brought with them earth taken from subterranean mountains. They used this earth to form the four sacred mountains that define the Navajo homeland: Hesperus Peak in Colorado's San Juan Mountains forming the northern limit, Mount Blanca in south-central Colorado forming the eastern edge, Mount Taylor in New Mexico forming the southern boundary, and the San Francisco Peaks, remnants of an ancient volcano in Flagstaff, marking the western border.

During the 1860s, Kit Carson was employed by the U.S. government to put an end to Navajo raiding. He starved the Navajos into surrender by killing their livestock and burning their crops, and then he marched the 8,000 prisoners across 300 miles to Bosque Redondo in southeastern New Mexico. For many Navajos the humiliation of defeat was compounded by the knowledge that they were being taken beyond the perimeter of the land defined by their sacred mountains. Since they believed that the religious chants central to their well-being would be ineffective away from their homeland, not only were they separated from their homes, they also felt separated from their gods.

In 1868, after being held prisoners for nearly five years, they signed a treaty agreeing never to fight again. They were allowed to return to their homeland, which then became a reservation. After leaving Bosque Redondo, one Navajo leader later recalled, "When we saw the top of the [sacred] mountain from Albuquerque, we wondered if it was our mountain, and we felt like talking to the ground, we loved it so, and some of the old men and women cried with joy . . . ."

While much has changed over the years in the homeland of both Navajos and Hopis, some conditions remain unchanged. Survival and water remain inextricably linked. Employment opportunities remain relatively scarce. Uranium mines, once a source of great controversy, illness, and death in the area, are gone, replaced by the massive Peabody coal mine on Black Mesa and a new controversy over that operation's competition for dwindling water resources.

The mine's thirst for water angers the Hopis, though the tribe derives several millions of dollars each year in royalties for the coal extracted. Navajos also benefit from the mine but are not as concerned about the water use because the much larger Navajo Reservation has other water sources available.

There are conflicts and vicissitudes in any community and culture, but all of this, in the region sometimes called Indian Country, is dwarfed by a single dominant feature — a landscape of dazzling color, clear skies, and dramatic cliffs and canyons. The late afternoon sun will always turn remnants of the plateau's monuments from golden to the deep red in the heart of a juniper log, and a half hour after sunset, the sky will fade to pink at the horizon, gradually yielding to deeper and deeper blue.

When night falls, it all disappears. Gone are the mesas and buttes, the rippled red sands, the short round hogans of the Navajos, and the stone houses on the Hopis' arid mesas. Without any light from a big city, only the blackest night and the brightest stars remain.

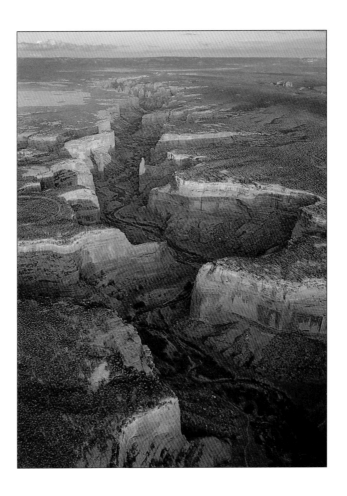

In the high, dry, burnt-red land of northeastern Arizona, erosion has carved countless canyons — some monumental, some small and intimate. (ABOVE) An aerial view shows the extent of Canyon de Chelly National Monument, where Ancestral Puebloan Indians farmed the canyon floor and built cliff houses a millennium ago. Today you can tour the canyon by four-wheel drive guided by the Navajo who live in the canyon. ADRIEL HEISEY

(RIGHT) A beam of light plays in a narrow slot canyon near Lake Powell. Slot canyons can seem almost subterranean because they are so narrow at the top. Water cut the original channels in the sandstone, and wind chiseled the rock's wavelike curves. MICHAEL FATALI

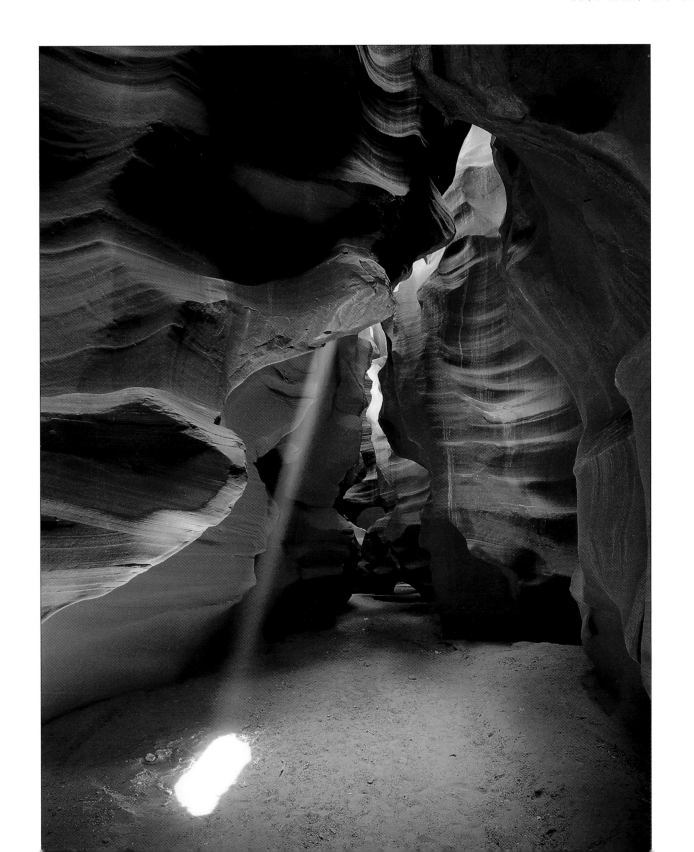

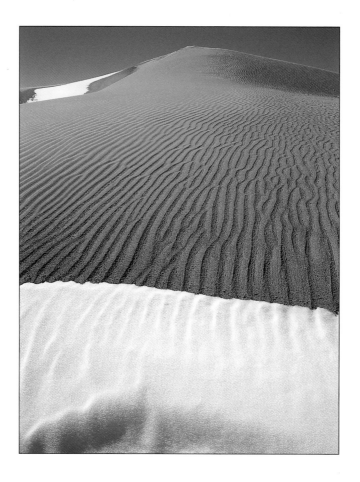

Called the Painted Desert for its multicolored sand dunes and rock formations, these vast badlands stretch for more than 100 miles across the Navajo and Hopi Indian reservations.
(ABOVE) Wind, snow, sunlight, and shadow combine to decorate the sand dunes of the western Painted Desert.
GEORGE H.H. HUEY
(RIGHT) Snow melts quickly on the sunlit sands but remains in the cool shadows of the eroded hills near Lupton.
ADRIEL HEISEY

(FOLLOWING PANEL, PAGES 32 AND 33) The otherworldly landscape viewed from Hunt's Mesa includes the eroded buttes, spires, and mesas of Little Monument Valley in the foreground and Monument Valley beyond. KERRICK JAMES

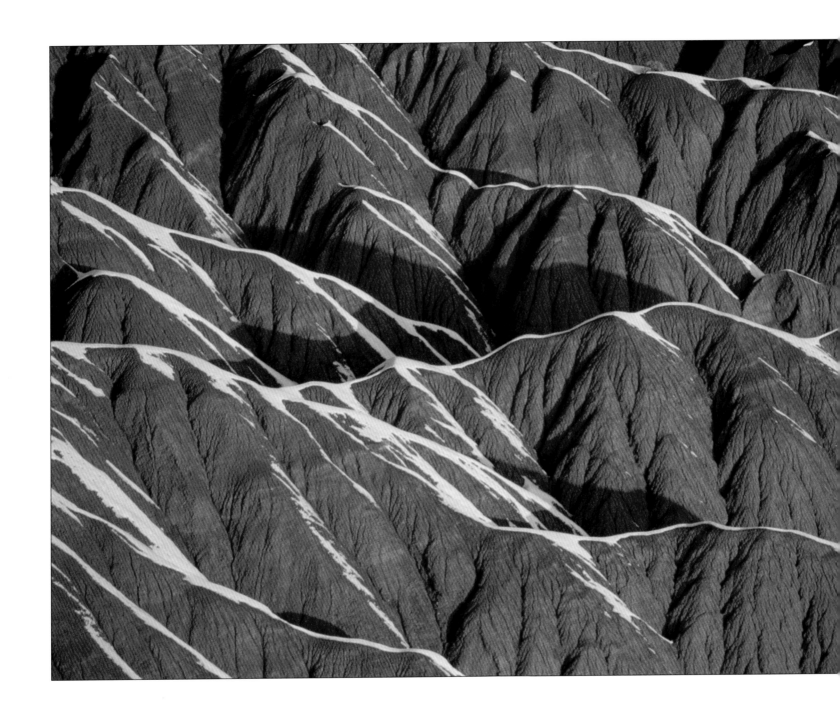

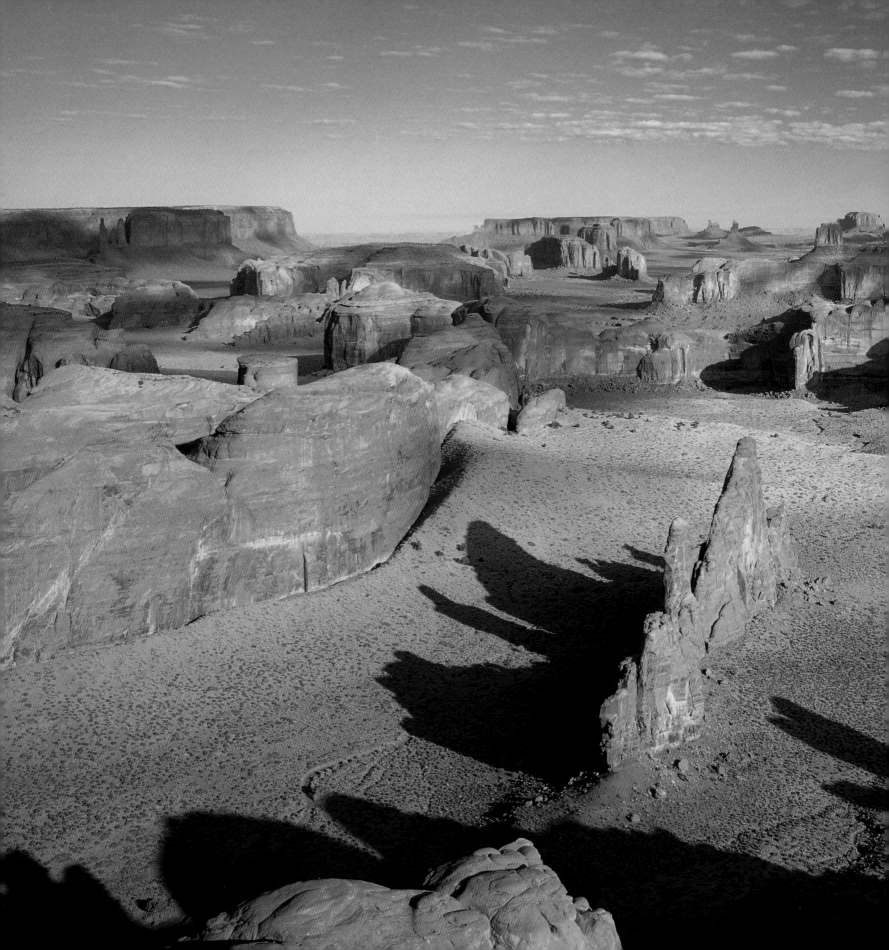

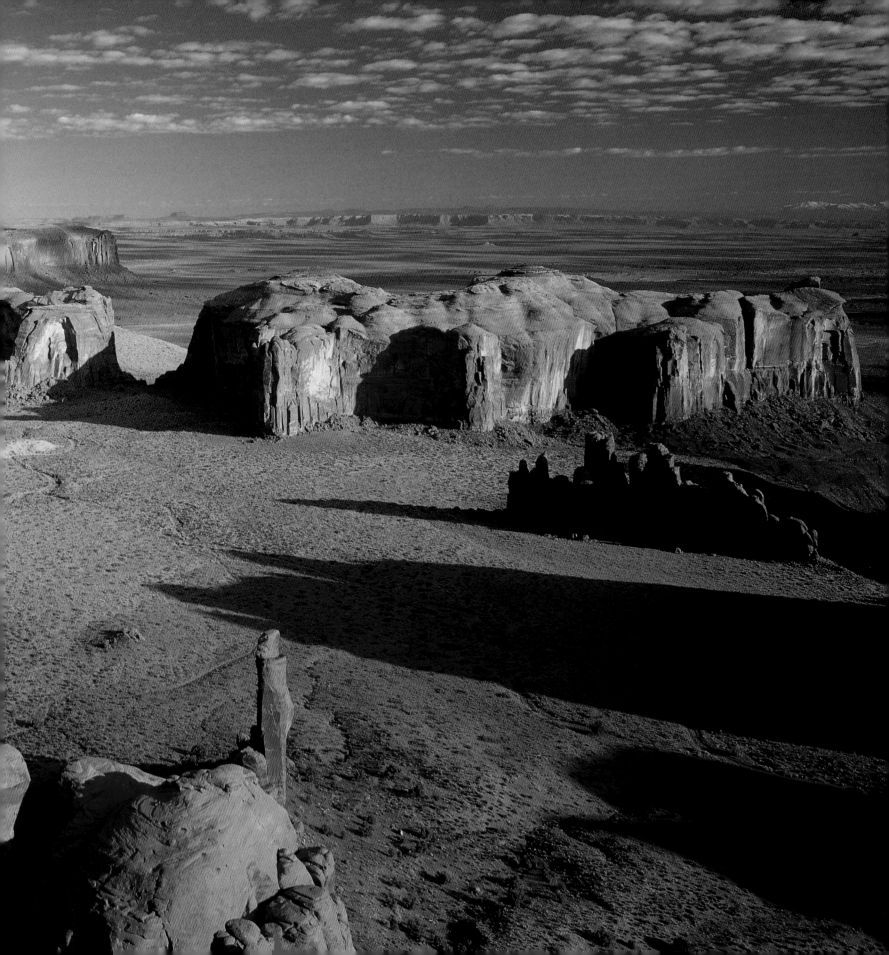

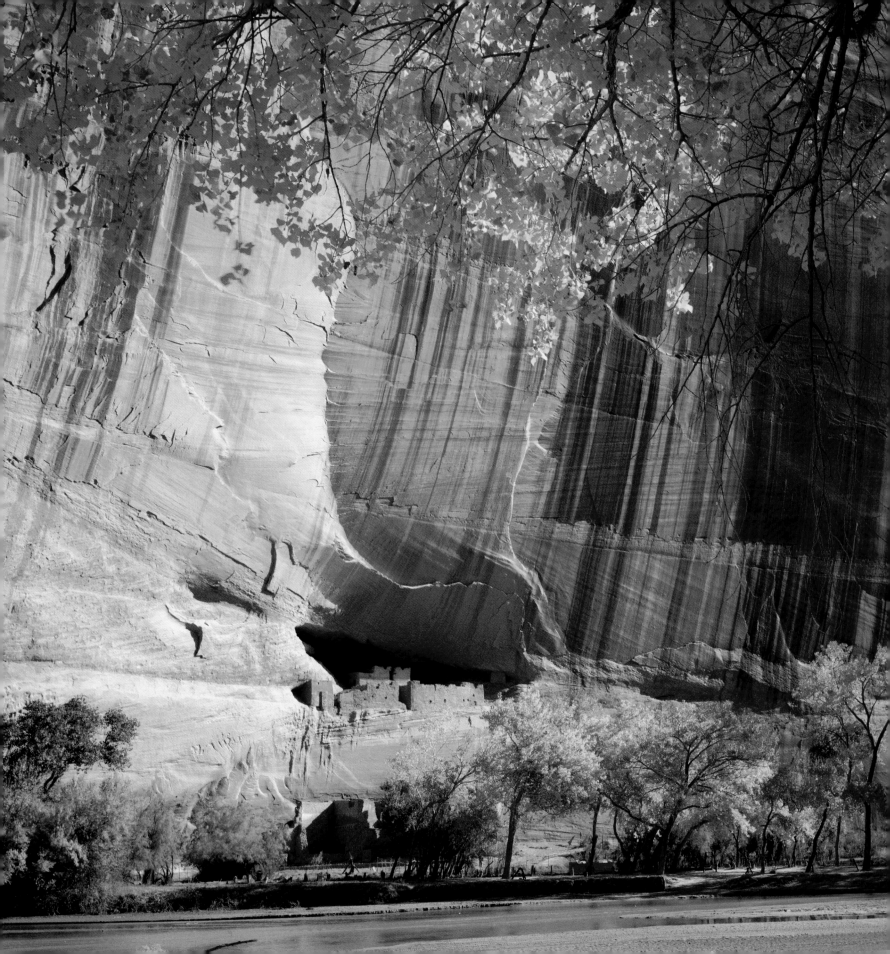

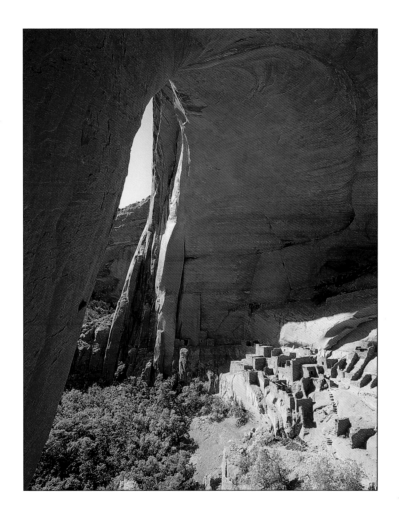

The Ancestral Puebloan, the ancient ones, thrived in the canyons of the Four Corners region of the Southwest about a thousand years ago, building their apartment-like cliff dwellings in south-facing alcoves to take advantage of warm sunlight in winter and cool shade in summer.

(LEFT) Canyon de Chelly's White House Ruin overlooks the fertile canyon bottom as it has for more than 700 years. DICK DIETRICH
(ABOVE) The well-hidden Betatakin Ruin was one of the last major Ancestral Puebloan ruins to be discovered in Arizona. GEORGE H.H. HUEY

(FOLLOWING PANEL PAGES 36 AND 37) Lake Powell, impounded behind Glenn Canyon Dam on the Colorado River is often referred to as "Monument Valley with water." MICHAEL FATALI

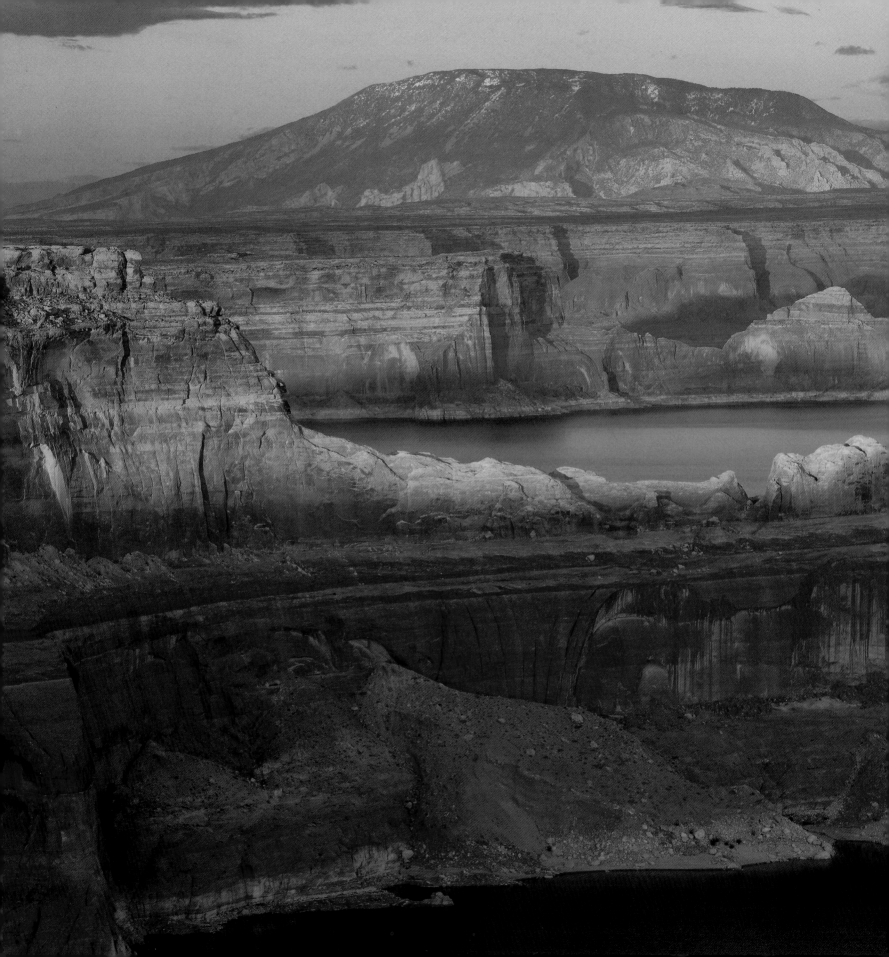

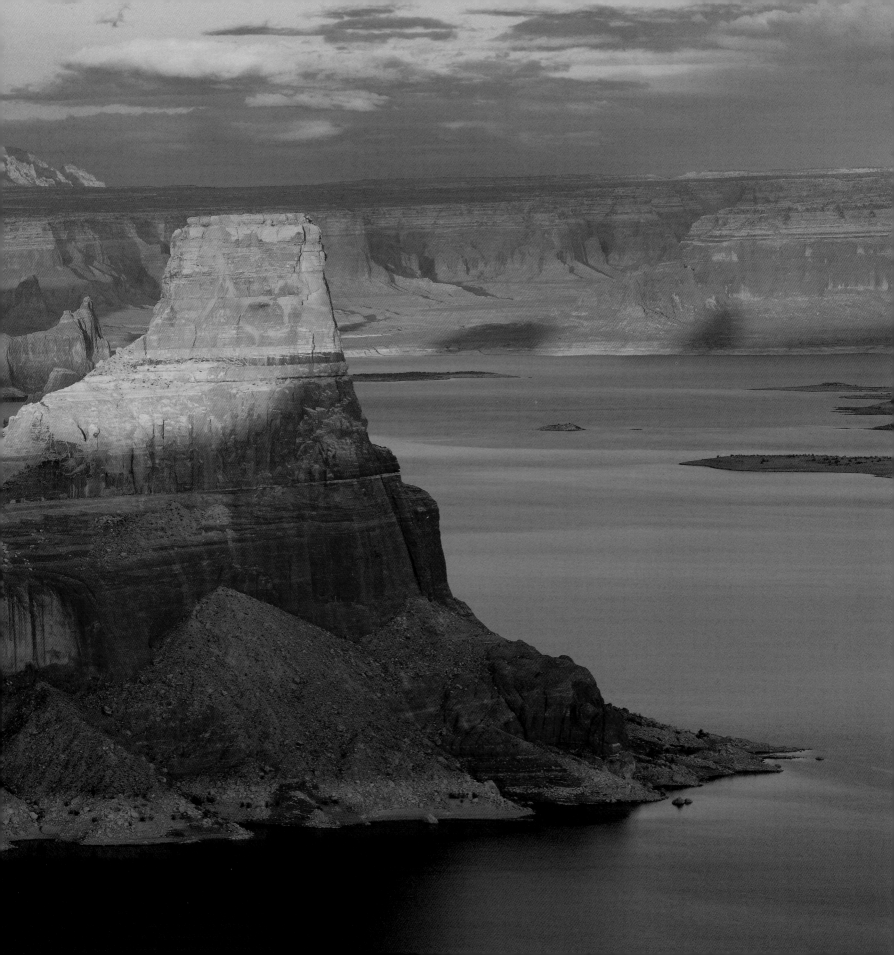

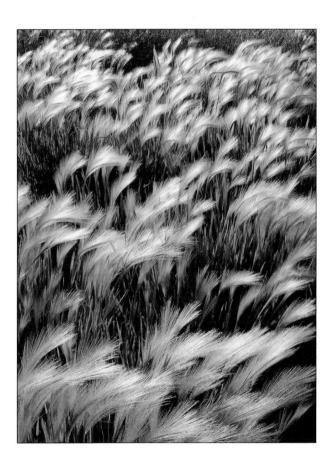

Indian Country is not all high desert, but has its verdant enclaves where abundant rainfall brings lush grass and forests.

(ABOVE) A wet spring turns the high desert into grasslands near Kayenta. GARY LADD

(RIGHT) Aspens surround a small lake in the remote Chuska Mountains along the Arizona-New Mexico state line. JERRY SIEVE

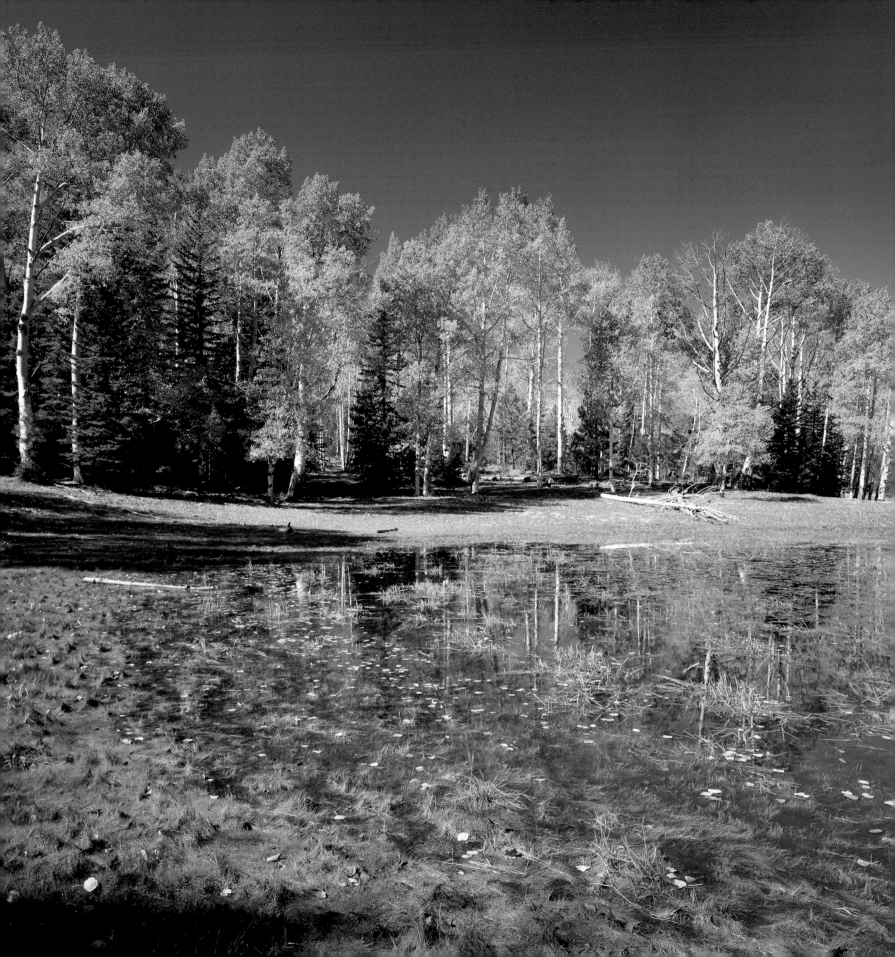

MOUNTAINS

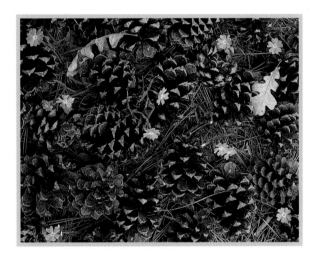

Ponderosa pine cones and Woodhouse's phlox in flower dot the Coconino National Forest floor.
JACK DYKINGA

thick with white-barked aspen at the base of the San Francisco Peaks on the outskirts of Flagstaff. About 30 feet from me, three deer stood still. The youngest was very curious about this creature opposite who managed to remain upright on only two feet, but it couldn't get a good look at me because a thin branch partially obscured its line of sight. It dipped its head to see below the branch.

On a whim, I bent my knees and dipped my head a bit, too. That caught its attention. It stretched its neck and peered over the top of the branch to get a better look. I stretched my neck and stared back. We kept this up for about five minutes until the yearling figured out that this flexible, two-legged accordion was odd, but not dangerous. Walking so lightly on its thin legs that I doubt it left a hint of a hoof print in the dark soil, it stepped away through the bell-shaped orange leaves that lay scattered in the forest like shards of stained-glass.

Years ago, in another mountain range in central Arizona, I had a discussion with a black bear. This bear had followed my son to our campsite a few hundred feet above the Black River. My son was frightened; the bear was, too. I clapped my hands above my head, and it moved off some 50 feet, rose on its hind legs, and struck a pathetic pose. I don't believe in regarding animals as humans, but since this one was 50 feet away and the safety of my truck was about two feet away, I decided to give it a piece of advice: "Leave." It sniffed the air for what seemed like an eternity and then disappeared into the folds of the White Mountains.

Mountains are the magic of central Arizona. The tallest — well over 12,000 feet high — tower over Flagstaff and cascade like a fountain of lava that rises and falls, forming pine- and spruce-covered peaks eastward to Show Low, Lakeside, Pinetop, and Greer, dipping into deep canyons and fording clear streams all the way to Mount Baldy and Escudilla Mountain near the New Mexico line. To the people who live on the Colorado Plateau to the north and the vast deserts of the south, these mountains are a special gift, a haven from searing summers when temperatures in the lower elevations often will exceed 100 degrees.

For me, the encounters with four-legged creatures reflect the size and quality of the habitat in that band of mountains forming a broken wall through central Arizona. Such encounters are not possible in populated areas, yet at times I've been surprised to see how closely the deer and elk live to busy population centers. At places like Terry Flat, a stunning alpine meadow near the top of Escudilla Mountain, it is not at all surprising to encounter elk or bear, since the nearest human settlements are small and widely scattered. But they're also found at Schultz Pass and in the woods off Snow Bowl Road, both just a few miles from the busy center of Flagstaff.

The Schultz Pass area, like most of the extraordinary wild country across the central part of the state, is in a national forest. The Prescott, Coconino, Kaibab, Apache, Tonto, and Sitgreaves national forests protect approximately 8.5 million acres of prime wildlife habitat and recreational land.

Scattered among these densely forested mountains are some of Arizona's most popular smaller communities. Prescott and Sedona, for example, are often regarded as the jewels of central Arizona, and with good reason.

Prescott, the first capital of territorial Arizona, is located only a couple of hours northwest of Phoenix, but it looks and feels like a small city in New England. The town, in fact, was designed by New Englanders dispatched by President Lincoln to establish the territorial government.

Situated at an altitude of 5,000 feet, Prescott's climate is relatively mild in summer and winter. Summer days are warm but not searing, and the nights are cool. Trees lining streets of Victorian homes put on a colorful display in the fall, and winters usually see some snow, but seldom enough to turn the residents into hermits. Flatlanders from Phoenix and its surrounding desert love to spend part of each summer in Prescott.

Prescott likes to think of itself as "Everybody's Home Town," an artifact of the 1950s where Ozzie and Harriet might be comfortable. It's a city with the cozy, inviting feel of a kitchen filled with the fragrance of freshly baked bread.

Sedona, on the other hand, is not so much cozy as it is dramatic, a place that, once seen, is never forgotten. Sedona, at 4,400 feet elevation, lies in a bowl at the bottom of Oak Creek Canyon, about 100 miles north of Phoenix. Though the main streets are lined with art galleries, gift shops, and tourist facilities, Sedona's chief attraction is its natural beauty. Striking red buttes, pinnacles, spires, and domes rise above it like a sanctuary for mythical gods, though in reality it has long been a haven not for gods but for artists and writers and retirees. In the 1920s Zane Grey made the area famous with his book, *Call of the Canyon,* which became a movie

shot amid the towering cliffs. These sandstone cliffs and rugged formations — with names like Snoopy, Bell Rock, Cathedral Rock — are not red as in apple red, but they change colors throughout the day, from pink to magenta to purple.

East of Sedona, the Coconino National Forest covers the top of the Mogollon Rim. The Tonto National Forest protects the pine-covered hills near Payson where Zane Grey had a cabin for many years. Eastward to the White Mountains, the Apache-Sitgreaves National Forests surround the communities of Show Low, Lakeside, and Pinetop, towns settled by Mormons sent by Brigham Young in the late 1800s. In addition to their permanent residents, these towns — with their refreshing temperatures and many lakes — are popular summer retreats for desert dwellers from Phoenix and Tucson. In the winter, the desert people return to ski the slopes of Sunrise Ski Resort, an

enterprise of the White Mountain Apache Tribe.

Once east of the White Mountain communities, the mountains begin to look more like they looked when only the Apaches called the area home. Take away the paved roads and amenities installed by the Forest Service and the Apaches for campers and fishermen, and the terrain would appear wild, primitive, and challenging. Even so, today it remains prime habitat for black bears, mountain lions, elk, and deer.

Everyone who has camped or trekked in the mountains of east-central Arizona undoubtedly has a favorite spot. For me, that spot is a long meadow high on a mountain some 10 miles north of Alpine. It was mid-July the first time I saw Terry Flat, and my first thought was that the place's name was singularly nondescript. Terry Flat, at an elevation of 9,500 feet, is a huge meadow shaped like a shallow bowl, and on that day it was a bowl filled with short grass and a mosaic of small violet, red, and yellow wildflowers.

The meadow was named for Lewis K. Terry, a rancher who lived a few miles southeast of Alpine during the 1920s and grazed his cattle in the high meadow that forms a shoulder just east of Escudilla.

Escudilla, which at 10,955 feet is the third-tallest peak in Arizona, is probably one of the least visited. Not only is it remote, but heavy snows make it practically impenetrable in the winter.

Aldo Leopold, a forest ranger and pioneer conservationist, believed the last grizzly bear in Arizona met its end in this lonesome terrain. Leopold chronicled the bear's death in his book, *A Sand County Almanac*, a collection of essays on nature published in 1949.

The last grizzly in Arizona was called Bigfoot. He was a ragged old bear, and he favored the high country up around Terry Flat and Escudilla Mountain on the Arizona-New Mexico line. This bear had good taste. Once a year, he'd eat a cow; the rest of the time he slept or wandered in a spruce- and aspen-covered paradise where — even today — he would have plenty of privacy.

A federal trapper had been called in to rid the area of livestock-killing predators. Here's Leopold's account of what happened next:

"The trapper packed his mule and headed for Escudilla. In a month he was back, his mule staggering under a heavy hide. There was only one barn in town big enough to dry it on. He had tried traps, poison and all his usual wiles to no avail. Then he had erected a set-gun in a defile through which only the bear could pass, and waited. The last grizzly walked into the string and shot himself."

There are those who might welcome the departure of the last grizzly in this country, but Aldo Leopold was not among them. In his essay about the killing, he wrote:

"Since the beginning, time had gnawed at the basaltic hulk of Escudilla, wasting, waiting and building. Time built three things on the old mountain: a venerable aspect, a community of minor animals and plants, and a grizzly.

"The government trapper who took the grizzly knew he had made Escudilla safe for cows. He did not know he had toppled the spire off an edifice a-building since the morning stars sang together."

From Escudilla Mountain southward to Hannagan Meadow, K.P. Cienega, and the Blue River, the story is one of uncommon isolation, deep forests of aspens, spruce, wild berries, and high meadows filled with ferns and wild irises in the summer. In this enormous corridor that extends, roughly, from Prescott to the New Mexico line, the human intrusion remains dwarfed by one precipitous mountain or canyon after another. Humans with their fishing poles and camping gear come and go in this vast terrain, but the mountains and their wildlife remain, providing continuity in a world where everything else is changing.

43

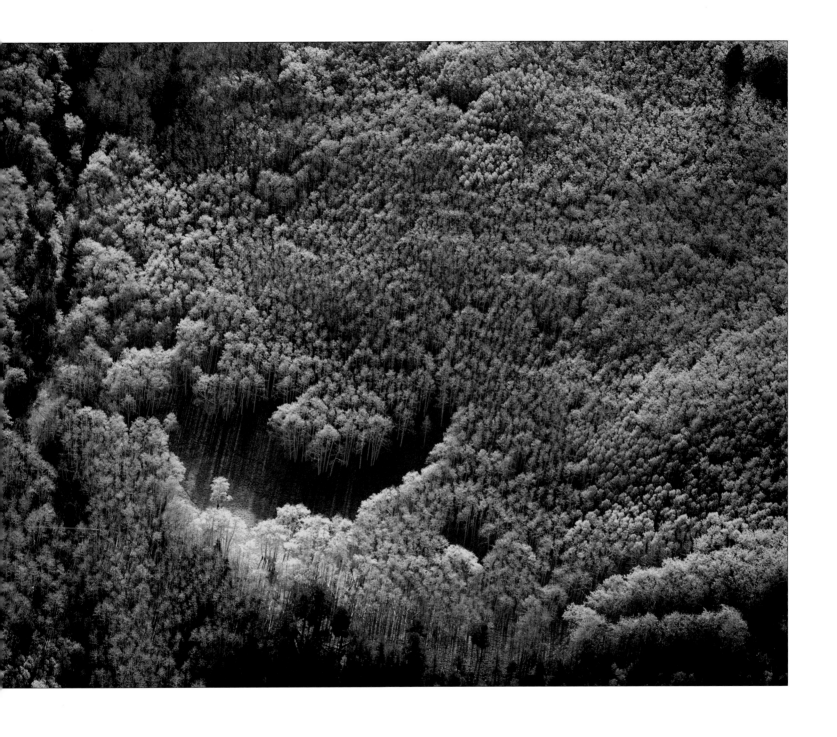

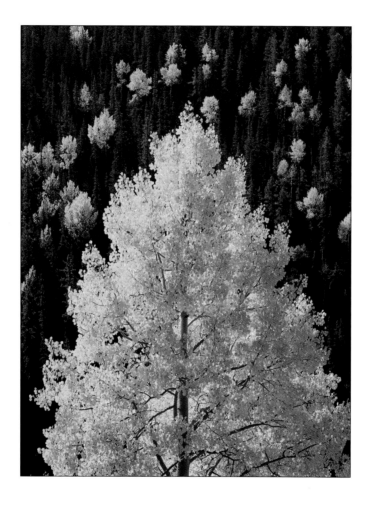

(LEFT) An aerial view of the extensive aspen groves on the San Francisco Peaks highlights the variation of color as autumn sweeps across the high country. MICHAEL COLLIER (ABOVE) In the White Mountains of eastern Arizona, aspens are found sprinkled throughout the forest as well as growing in dense groves. RANDY PRENTICE

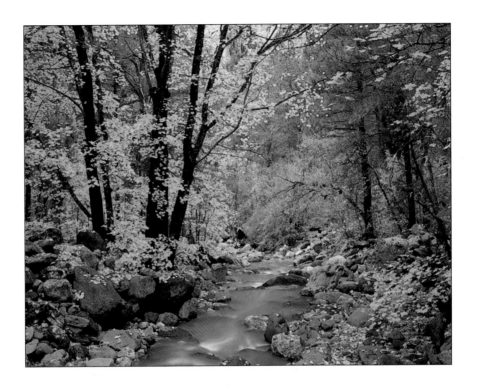

Rugged, scenically spectacular canyons cut the sheer face of the Mogollon Rim, a massive escarpment that runs diagonally across much of central Arizona. Two of the better-known canyons, Oak Creek and Sycamore, lie side by side in the red rock country near Sedona, but provide different experiences for the outdoorsperson. A highway leads past cabins and resorts in Oak Creek Canyon, while Sycamore is a designated Forest Service Wilderness where only a rocky trail leads to Nature's glories.

(ABOVE) Autumn maples glow in Oak Creek Canyon.
BOB & SUZANNE CLEMENZ
(RIGHT) Prickly pear cactuses sprout from the cliffs above the verdant, spring-fed south end of Sycamore Canyon.
GEORGE H.H. HUEY

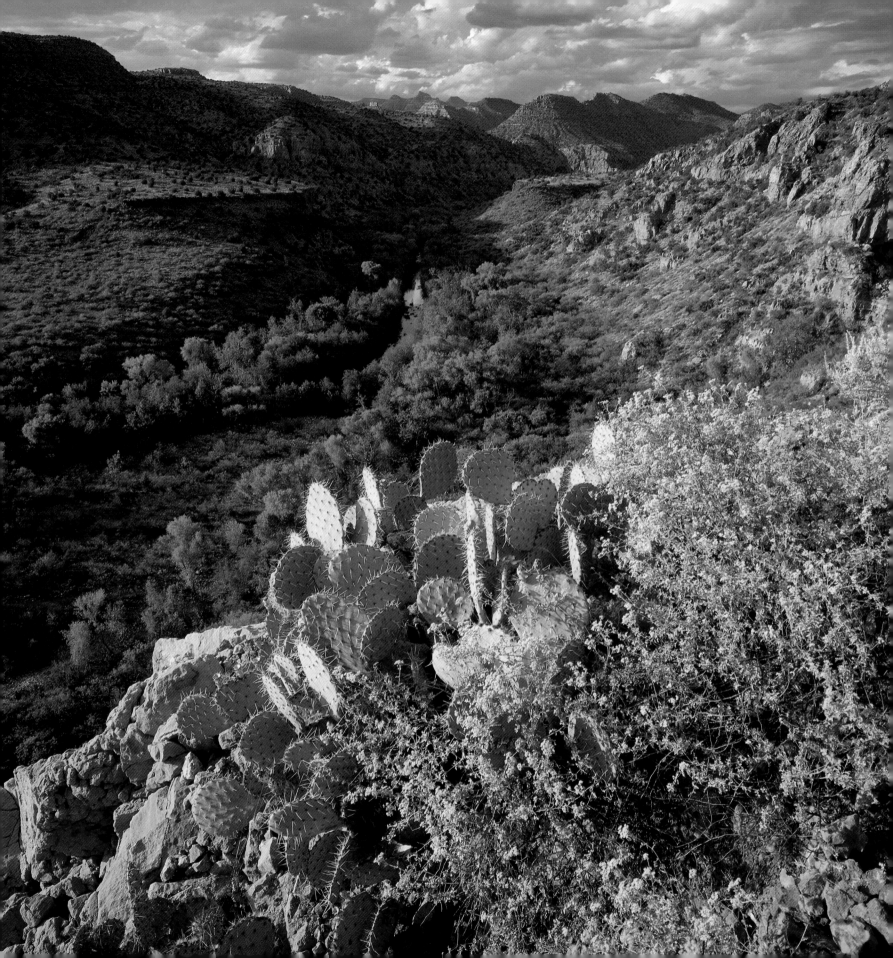

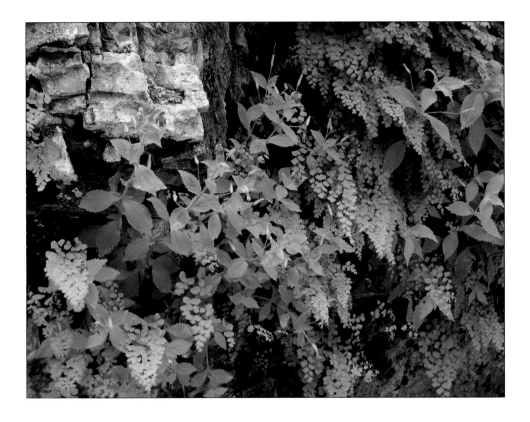

One of the Mogollon Rim's more beautiful and lush wilderness canyons takes its name and moisture from sparkling West Clear Creek, which is fed by numerous springs along its more than 40-mile course.

(ABOVE) Monkey flowers cling to West Clear Creek Canyon's sheer cliffs.
(RIGHT) A travertine spring creates Hanging Gardens before adding its waters to West Clear Creek.
BOTH BY NICK BEREZENKO

(FOLLOWING PANEL, PAGES 50 AND 51) The waters of the Verde River cascade below Horseshoe Reservoir.
LONNA TUCKER

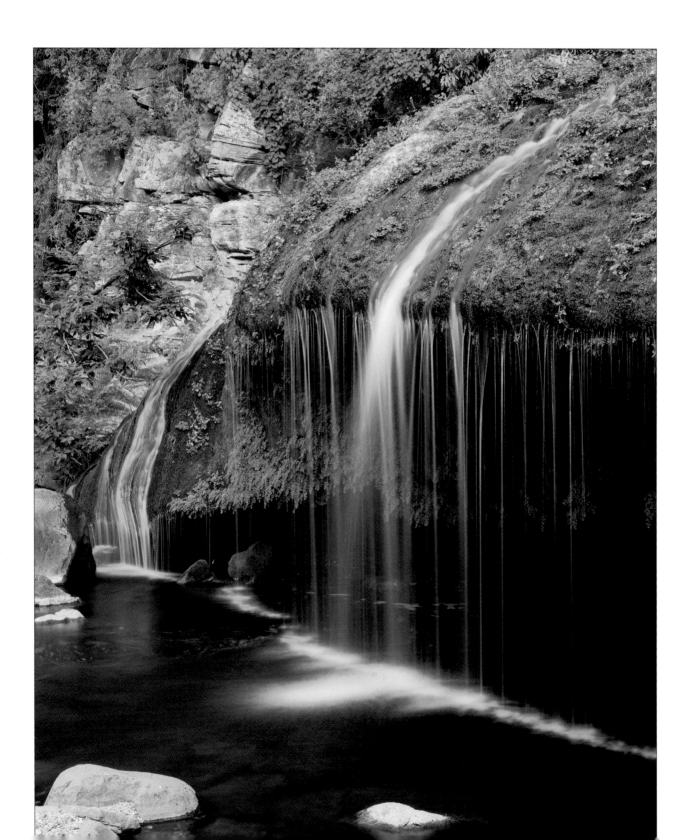

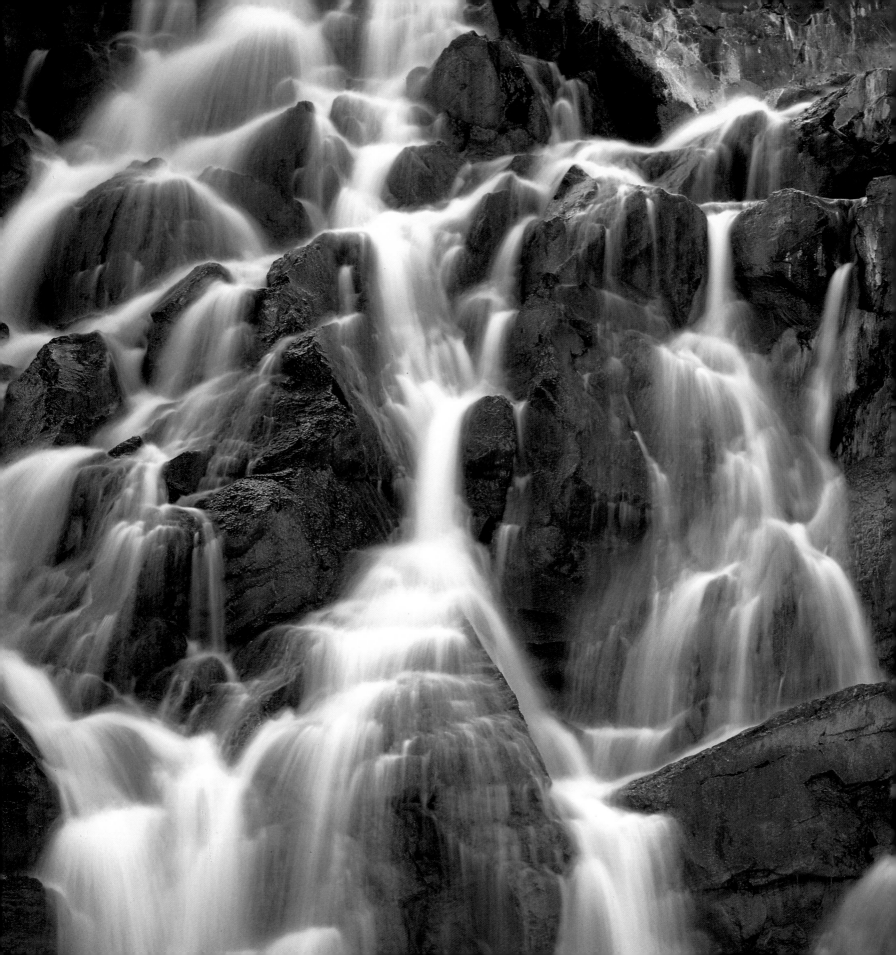

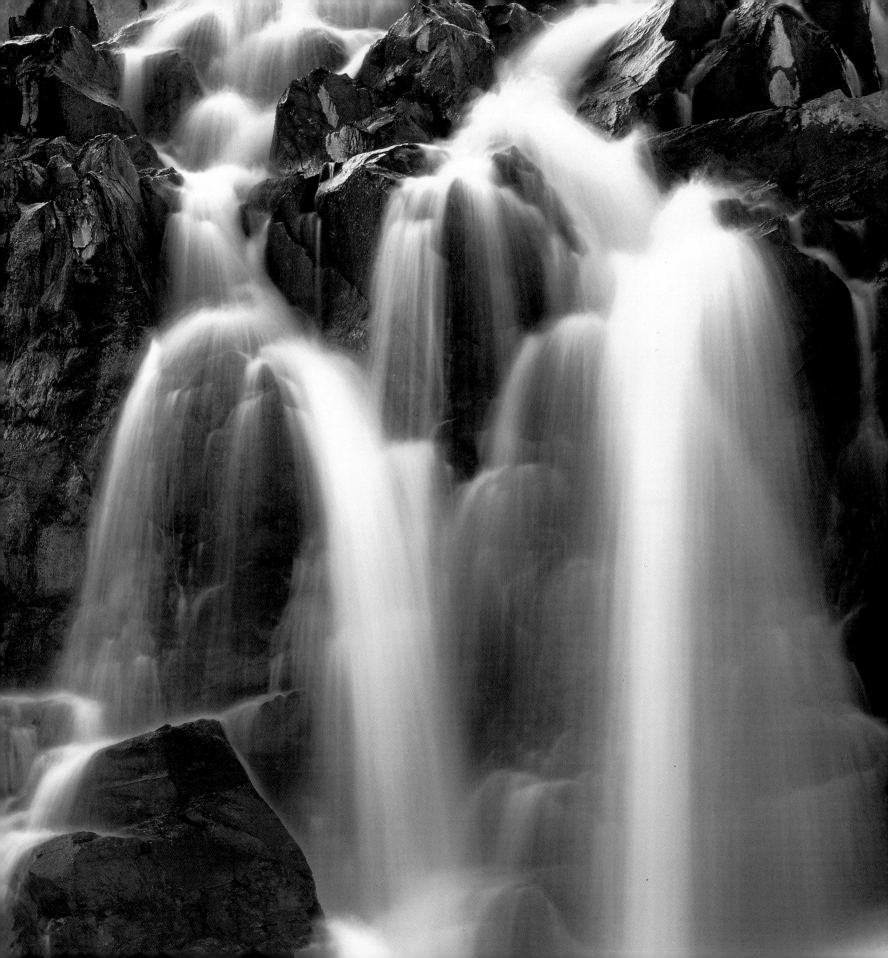

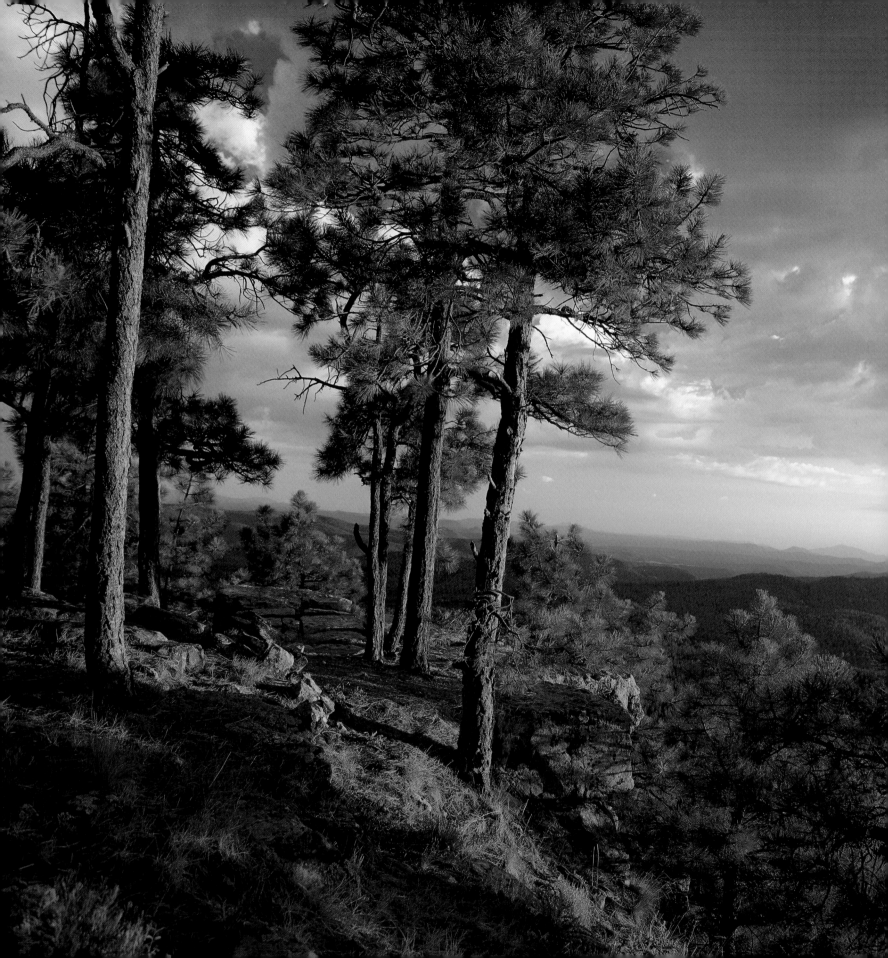

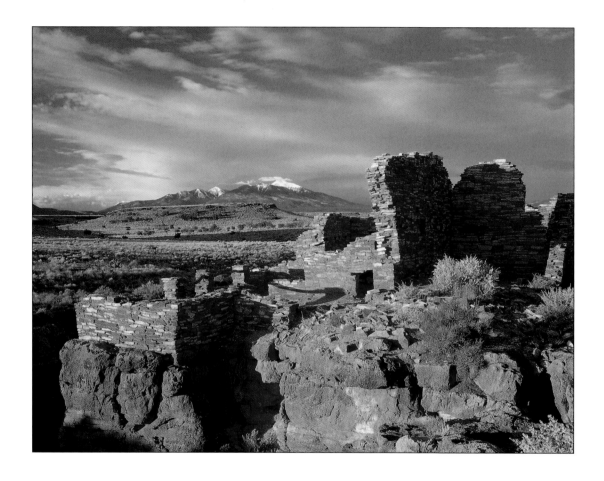

People have found Arizona's forested Mogollon Rim and high country a hospitable home since the beginning of time.

(LEFT) The Mogollon Rim defines the southern side of the Colorado Plateau.
DICK DIETRICH
(ABOVE) Lomaki Ruin, a Sinagua culture dwelling at

Wupatki National Monument northeast of Flagstaff, stands before the San Francisco Peaks as it has for more than 700 years. TOM DANIELSEN

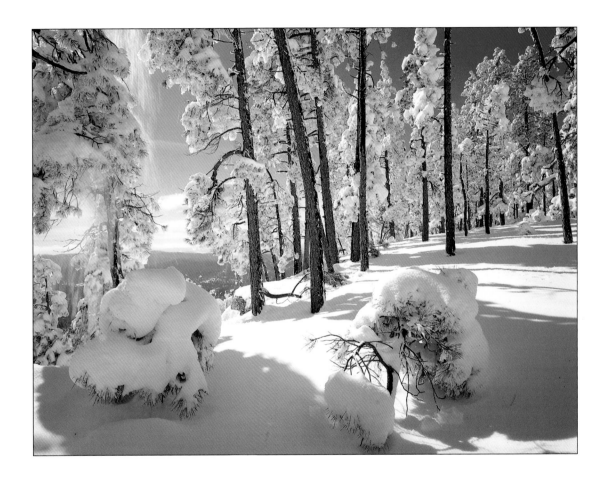

(ABOVE) Deep snows often blanket the forest atop the Mogollon Rim at Al Fulton Point. JERRY SIEVE

(RIGHT) Below the Rim a light frosting of snow occasionally dusts the buttes and monuments of red rock country such as Coffee Pot Rock, near Sedona.
BOB & SUZANNE CLEMENZ

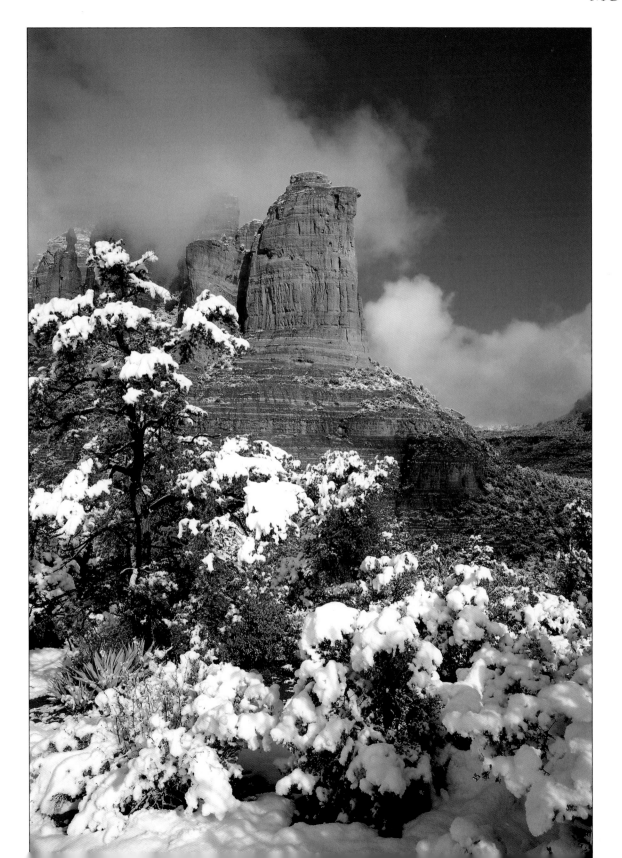

WESTERN ARIZONA

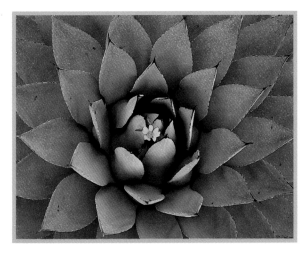

Soil deposited in an agave by desert winds provides a perfect environment for a wild flower.
DAVID MUENCH

I was halfway up Palm Canyon in the Kofa Mountains, about 60 miles north of Yuma in western Arizona. It was a weekday and until the bird called out, I had heard only the wind and my breath and, from time to time, the loose rocks underfoot. Western Arizona is heavily visited but not heavily populated. Drive away from any town on the Colorado River, and a landscape of deep solitude is less than an hour away.

On that bright winter morning, with not another human visible, the Kofas struck me as strange and eerie: rhyolite sand castles formed by the trembling earth 25 million years ago, the ridge lines looking like an upheaval of giant dinosaur teeth protruding from the backs of reclining amphibians. Like most of western Arizona, the Kofas are lucky to get six inches of rainfall in an entire year. Six inches — not much more than a glass of water for every plant and animal. That anything whatsoever grows in this rocky fastness seems miraculous.

I had gone to Palm Canyon to see one of those miracles: in a place where most trees and bushes seldom grow as tall as an average human, a thick grove of tall native palm trees thrived. In a narrow cut off the main canyon, I crossed a boulder-strewn wash and looked up at the wild palms that gave the place its name.

Most botanists think this strange community, some 40 or 50 California fan palms tucked into a steep and rocky fissure, may represent the only wild native palms in Arizona. There are others who think these trees are not native to the area but merely grew from seeds carried in the digestive tracts of coyotes and other free-roaming creatures. The debate didn't interest me. The spectacle did. A glass of water for everything else in the area, but here, clearly, was a microclimate that enabled palm trees to grow tall. Because palm trees do not produce growth rings like shade trees, no one knows how long these trees have been around.

When I heard, in the fall of 1995, that the Walt Disney studio was considering the Yuma area as a location to shoot a new movie about life on another planet, I was not surprised. Much of the terrain looks as lifeless as Mars. Names such as the Chocolate Mountains, the Trigo Mountains (*trigo* means "wheat" in Spanish), the Castle Dome Mountains, and the Dome Rock Mountains reflect the colors and shapes that dominate this unusual landscape. The Kofa Mountains may be one exception: the name is an acronym for King of Arizona, a now-dormant gold and silver mine.

A barren expanse of sandy hills where summer temperatures will often reach 120 degrees and more, western Arizona is where Gen. George Patton trained his tank troops for fighting in the Sahara Desert during World War II. The army still tests its heavy artillery at the Yuma Proving Ground.

Only two ingredients have modified the harshness of this terrain: the human imagination and the Colorado River, a finicky stream dubbed by one inventive promoter as "The American Nile."

The north end of Yuma, the city's oldest section, is a good example of how an inhospitable landscape can be transformed by the imagination. At the turn of the century an Italian immigrant named E. F. Sanguinetti settled here and became the city's most prominent businessman. Sanguinetti clearly had the soul of a poet, but he lived in a place where temperatures were unbearable, where the river flooded almost every year, and where people survived misery by burning manure to ward off mosquitoes. So, what did Sanguinetti do? He retreated to his backyard (now the site of a restaurant) and turned it into the garden of an Italian villa: he planted purple bushes of bougainvillea, groves of bamboo, orange trees, a giant guamuchil tree, and languorous palms, and then he built aviaries for his cockatiels and doves.

I sat in this garden in December, forgetting about the tawny sands and muddy Colorado nearby. For a while, I wanted to be a character in an old black-and-white movie filmed at an oasis along the Nile. (Numerous movies have been filmed in or near Yuma since 1926.) What brought on that nostalgia? I wondered. Was it the lazy late afternoon ambiance that lay just beyond this flowering oasis?

When I tell people — even Yuma natives — about my reaction to the old part of their city, they sometimes look at me perplexed. Hardly

58

anyone feels as comfortable as I do among those flat-topped adobe buildings, the narrow streets with store fronts that look 100 years old, the red-tipped ocotillos and bougainvillea softening the blinding sunlight.

Maybe the appeal is heightened because, when I first came to this town 25 years ago, I was prepared not to like it. I'd been warned that western Arizona was hot and ugly, but the people who made that warning did not know or did not appreciate the niches of beauty up and down the river. On that trip, I visited a Yuma writer, Rosalie Crowe, who lived in a horseshoe-shaped house with a verandah wrapped around an inner courtyard shaded by porches and graceful palms. I felt like a character in a Graham Greene novel. Where was my Panama hat?

Western Arizona is not like other places. It does not conform to conventional ideas about what constitutes beautiful scenery. As Rosalie Crowe and Sidney Brinckerhoff wrote in their book, *Early Yuma*, "Not even the Indians liked it well enough to make it a permanent home." The Quechan Indians farmed near the river in the winter but headed for the cool San Diego Mountains west of Yuma to escape the capricious floods and swarming mosquitoes during the searing summers. And yet this land has its own exotic appeal rooted in unpredictability and enhanced by the element of surprise.

The face of Arizona was carved over millions of years by volcanic eruptions, lava flows, wind, rain, and the grinding action of moving rocks. In most places, humans left their mark on the landscape, but in the strange sand-castle terrain of western Arizona, the chief architect was not a person. It was a muddy river laden with silt.

Most of the area is a part of the 119,000-square-mile Sonoran Desert and, if conventional wisdom prevailed, nothing would survive in this terrain; yet wildlife is abundant, much of it protected in three national wildlife refuges — the Kofa, Imperial, and Havasu. These are habitats for bighorn sheep, ring-tailed cats, several species of bats, those native palms, and — strangest of all — a huge population of sea birds that follow the Colorado northward from Mexico and the Gulf of California.

Until 1909 the Colorado River was a wide, wild stream that slipped gracefully through Glen Canyon on the Utah-Arizona border, plunged some 200 miles south and west through the narrow gorges of Grand Canyon, then chewed its way south again through the barren deserts and fudge-colored mountains separating Arizona from both Nevada and California. The river flowed past Bullhead City, Parker, Lake Havasu City, was joined by the Gila River just north of Yuma, and then snaked southward across the fertile delta to its terminus in the Gulf of California (also known as the Sea of Cortez).

Between 1909 and 1938 the Colorado was gradually sedated by the construction of Laguna, Hoover, Imperial, and Parker dams. A levee was subsequently built along the east bank to protect irrigated farmlands south of Yuma; the water in the river that drains more than 90 percent of

Arizona's land mass then receded, and the Cocopah Indians who have lived in this region since around A.D. 1450 moved down to the red silt of the delta bottom.

In the 18th century the Spaniards looking for a route from Mexico through Arizona to California joined the Cocopah in this barren terrain. The river was the greatest impediment to the Spaniards' goal, but they found, with the help of the Cocopah and Yuma Indians familiar with its behavior, that the river could best be forded near Yuma in a place that came to be known as Yuma Crossing.

In 1849, prospectors heading for the California gold fields crossed the river at this point, following the route that Spanish soldiers and missionaries had traversed nearly a hundred years earlier. Yuma Crossing was included in the Gadsden Purchase from Mexico in 1854, making the site a part of the United States. Today Yuma Crossing is a state historic park with restored territorial buildings and covered wagons at the edge of the river in the north end of Yuma.

Yuma, located in the middle of a harsh desert, once was, ironically, a busy port city. From 1852 to 1909, shallow-draft steamboats operated from the Gulf of California to Yuma Crossing and points further north, carrying supplies and materials from California used to develop Arizona and New Mexico territories. The boat traffic eventually was replaced by the faster and more efficient railroads.

Now, the dammed-up river provides a haven for migrating sea birds, another anomaly in an area where one expects only a scorching desert.

The desert and river come together at the Imperial National Wildlife Refuge, some 20 miles north of Yuma. The refuge was established in 1949 to protect the diverse plant and animal life that inhabit both ecosystems. It is a great place of translucent backwater lakes where the only sounds are often the cry of gulls and the slap of a heron's feet on the water's glassy surface. The Sonoran Desert, hottest and driest desert in the United States, fills the distance, but in this spot along the river, willows

and the reedy shoreline harbor migratory fowl like Canada geese. You may see golden and bald eagles, whistling swans, or the black-crowned night heron, perhaps even a rare black rail.

It is a landscape that nurtures a most unusual combination of ingredients. Before the first dam was built in 1909, the river channel had a history of reshaping its route depending on the extent of floods caused by run-off and heavy rains.

Today the river is a tamed giant, used extensively by vacationers who enjoy wintertime temperatures in the 70s. Controlled releases of the Colorado's water from the dams to the north support huge groves of citrus, medjool dates, and miles of lettuce and broccoli fields near Yuma, creating a modern, sprawling Garden of Eden where native plants may get a glass of water for the entire year, and irrigated crops get all the water they need.

59

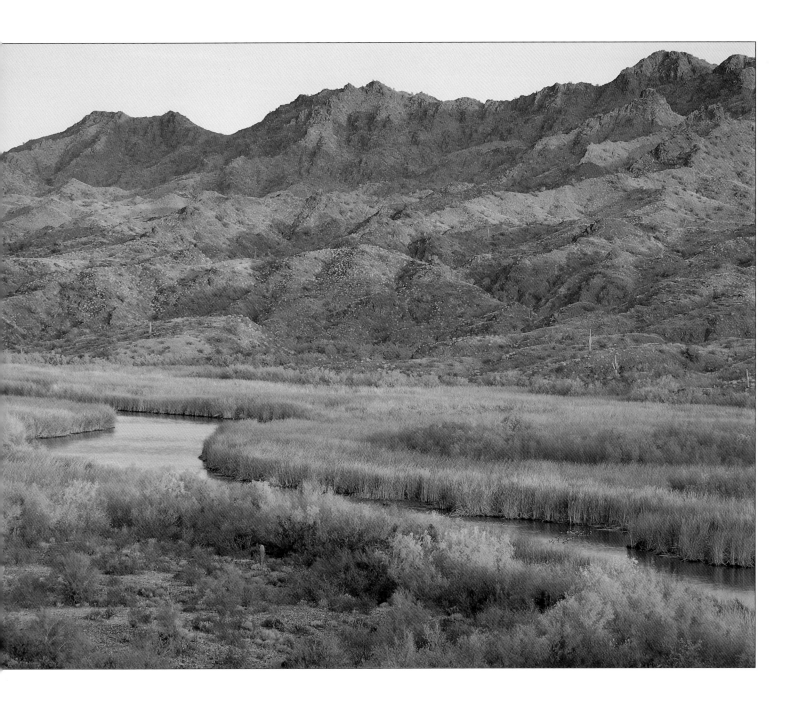

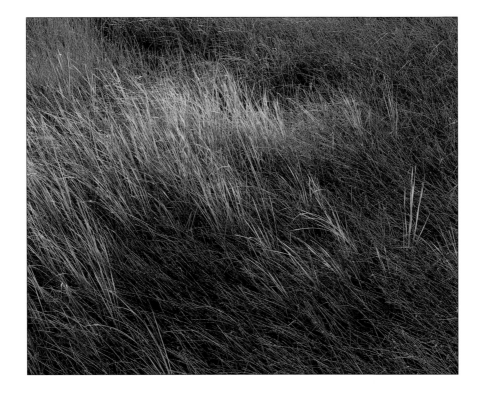

Sprinkled over the desert in western Arizona, the lush beauty of riparian habitats along waterways stands out in contrast to the starkness of the surrounding drylands. The cattail is a staple of such marshy areas. The reedy plant with long flat leaves often is used to make mats and chair seats.

(LEFT) Along the Bill Williams River in the Havasu National Wildlife Refuge, a marsh flourishes amid Sonoran Desert dryland vegetation. GEORGE H.H. HUEY

(ABOVE) Cattail mingles with bulrush in the Imperial National Wildlife Refuge along the Colorado River north of Yuma. JACK DYKINGA

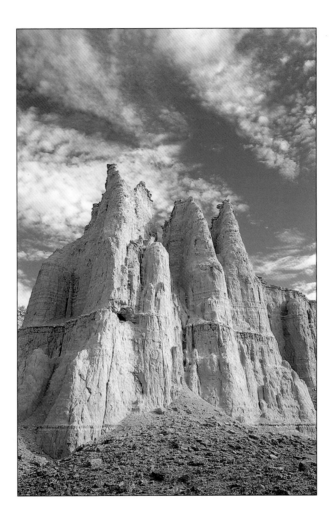

Unlike the impact of
waterways in other parts of
the world, the influence of
desert rivers wanes not far
from their banks.
(ABOVE) Near Wikieup, barely
50 miles east of the Colorado
River, eroded clay and sand
formations, sculpted over
eons, dominate the barren
landscape. STEVE BRUNO

(RIGHT) Even closer to the
river, the Black Mountains lie
at the northern end of the
Mohave Desert — at
approximately 40,000 square
miles, the smallest desert in
North America. The Mohave
also encompasses Death
Valley in California. JERRY JACKA

(FOLLOWING PANEL, PAGES 64
AND 65) At the lower end of
the Colorado River, the
Mohave Desert gives way to
the Yuma Desert and sand
dunes reminiscent of the
Sahara. DICK DIETRICH

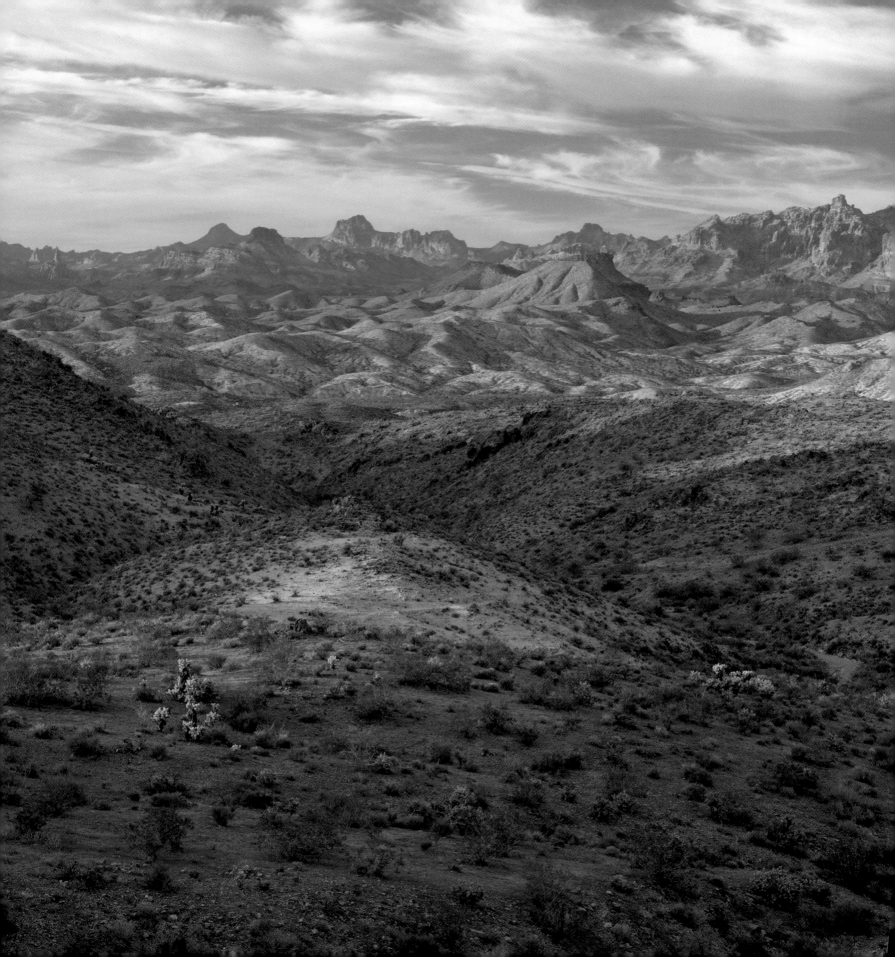

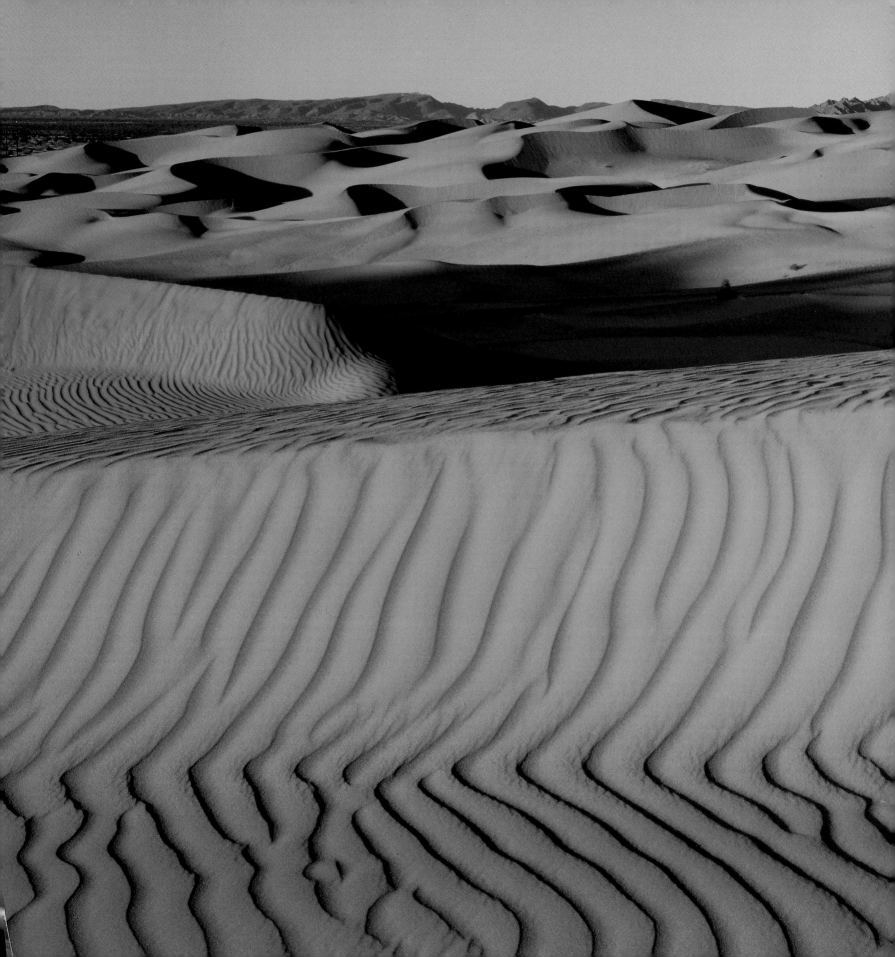

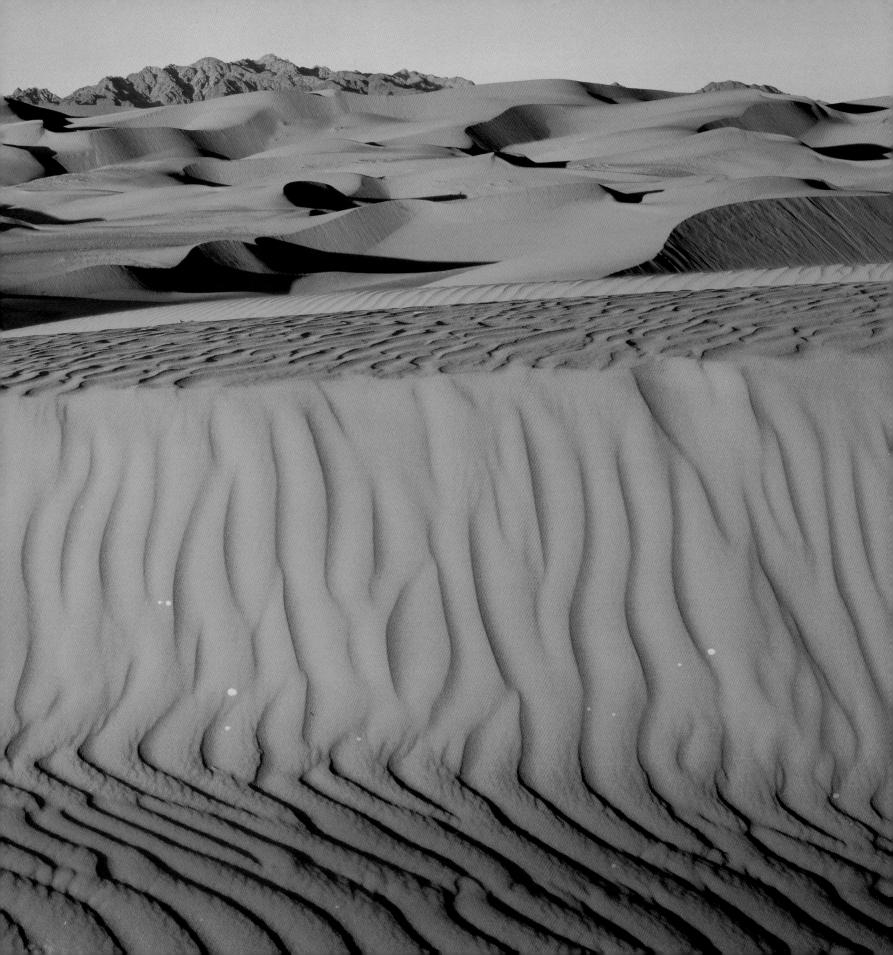

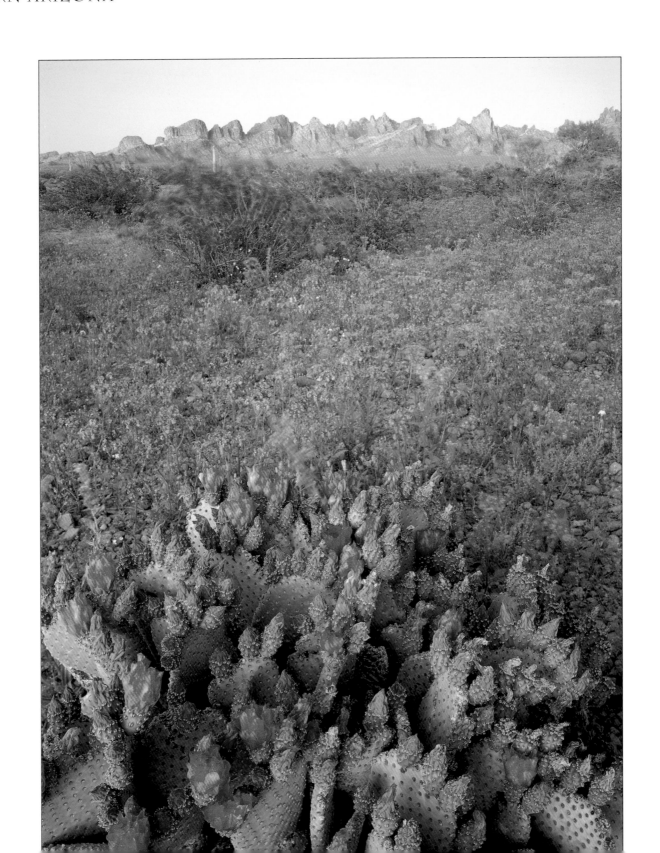

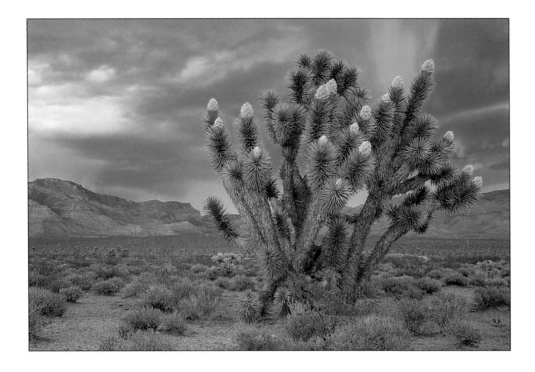

The combination of vegetation on slopes and plains and barren mountains yields a beauty based on contrast. (LEFT) Beavertail prickly pear cactus and scorpionweed flourish on an escarpment of the Kofa Mountains, a range of jagged volcanic pinnacles so foreboding that travelers avoided it for centuries. TOM TILL

(ABOVE) A Joshua tree, a member of the yucca family, is considered a marker of the Mohave Desert because it thrives primarily in that expanse. This Joshua blooms at the edge of the Beaver Dam Mountains in the far northwest sector of Arizona. Farther south, a portion of U.S. Highway 93 northwest of Phoenix wends through a forest of the yucca and is designated the Joshua Tree Parkway. STEVE BRUNO

SOUTHWESTERN DESERT

IN THE DESERTS OF SOUTHWESTERN ARIZONA, IT'S EASY TO DISAPPEAR.

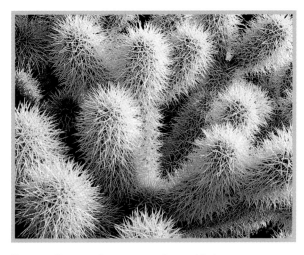

Dense silvery spines cover the teddy bear cactus, giving it the deceptively fuzzy appearance from which it draws its name. LAURENCE PARENT

Winds ripping across alkaline soils, lava rocks, and scant vegetation eventually eradicate most signs of human occupation. With little to block the long views across hundreds of miles, the few signs of life that remain can be overlooked easily. Jose Lorenzo Sestier, a Frenchman who crossed this terrain in the last century, was more fortunate than most. When he died in 1900 at a peaceful outpost called Quitobaquito, his employer installed an impressive gravestone to mark the hill where he was buried. I stumbled across the grave on a mild day in January while wandering the hilly desert near the man-made pond at Quitobaquito.

Quitobaquito is in Organ Pipe Cactus National Monument, but long before the site was made part of a national park, it was just one more tiny outpost where Sand Papago Indians, relatives of today's Tohono O'odham

Indians, had a few houses and a dependable water supply.

Unlike Sestier, many others who visited Quitobaquito — the record dates back to 1540 — slipped away without notice or memorial. Most of those who stopped to refresh themselves at Quitobaquito's springs were headed west to California, following a route near the Mexican border that came to be known as El Camino del Diablo, the Devil's Highway. Most of that route is now included in the 860,000-acre Cabeza Prieta National Wildlife Refuge. Cabeza Prieta, "dark head" in Spanish, refers to a granite-topped lava peak within the refuge.

El Camino del Diablo begins its 250-mile course in Caborca, a city in the Mexican state of Sonora. The route enters Arizona in the vicinity of Organ Pipe Cactus National Monument and turns west, roughly paralleling the Arizona-Mexico border until it reaches the Colorado River at Yuma. For roughly 200 years, from 1540 on, it was the shortest land route for Spanish explorers and missionaries headed for California. However, because it crossed a searing desert where the average rainfall is less than five inches per year, it was also a dangerous route.

Then as now, dependable springs were few and far between, and the Devil's Highway took its name from the many who died of thirst or starvation, leaving bleached bones scattered on the harsh land called malpais, sometimes within yards of the nearest water source.

Bill Broyles, a high school English teacher in Tucson who has spent many years traveling the area, noted: "Thirst was not the only difficulty … Marauders, lost routes, broken equipment,

and windstorms compounded the problems of reaching Yuma, let alone California. Virtually every written account of a trip across El Camino — even contemporary ones — chronicles some brush with disaster."

In a landscape where summertime temperatures reach 120 degrees and a human requires two gallons of water a day to survive, many a crude grave marker can be found.

Most of the graves along El Camino del Diablo can be found near the southern end of the Tinajas Altas Mountains, some 30 miles from the route's end at Yuma. The Tinajas Altas Mountains, "high tanks" in Spanish, are named for several large, natural depressions in the rocks above the Camino that collect rain water. But the tanks are not easy to reach and a number of travelers who had run out of water and were too weak or dehydrated

to make the climb to the tinajas died. Many of those travelers who met their fate on El Camino del Diablo were bound for the gold fields in California in the 1840s and 1850s. Their graves at or near Tinajas Altas provide grim evidence of the desert's harshness.

The southwestern Arizona desert, remarkably lush with vegetation at Organ Pipe (named for a cactus unique to the region), becomes a strange land of sand dunes, jagged lava, ash, and spiny vegetation farther west. It is a landscape that some, including Norwegian explorer Carl Lumholz, geographer Ronald L. Ives, naturalist Gary Paul Nabhan, and adventurous people like Bill Broyles, have found fascinating. It is intriguing, almost mysterious with deep arroyos, lichen-covered rocks, and sandy washes where coyotes, rattlesnakes, big-horn sheep,

70

jackrabbits, and javelina (a wild pig-like animal) are common. If winter rains have been plentiful, it is a land that will produce a striking array of wildflowers in the spring.

Quitobaquito, located about 100 feet from the international boundary with Mexico, is a shady, life-saving oasis in a place where the summer heat can be fatal, yet it did nothing for the imagination of one William T. Hornaday, a New York botanist who camped there during a 1908 expedition. In his expedition memoirs, *Camp-fires on Desert and Lava*, Hornaday wrote: "Although Quitovaquita [sic] was entirely quiet and inoffensive, its atmosphere was depressing. It is one of the spots in which I would not like to die, and would hate to live."

Others did not share Hornaday's opinion. Like any reliable watering hole in Arizona, Quitobaquito has a long history of human encounters. Melchior Diaz, a member of the Coronado expedition of 1540, probably stopped there. Jesuit missionary Father Eusebio Kino baptized Indian children near there around 1698 and described Quitobaquito simply as "a good place." Spanish explorer Juan Bautista de Anza passed it during the expedition of 1774-1775 to locate a passage to California. A man named Andrew Dorsey settled there in 1860 and dug the pond that is there today. Ten years later there was a store and gold mill at the pond, and Tohono O'odham Indians lived a quarter mile away. By the time the Hornaday expedition arrived, three Americans and their Indian wives were living at the site. Two years after the Hornaday party came through, the Norwegian naturalist and explorer Carl Lumholz rode into Quitobaquito looking for Cara Colorado (Red Face), a Tohono O'odham Indian he wanted to engage as a guide. Lumholz recorded this impression of the oasis:

"The tiny stream, fed by the springs, carries beautiful, limpid water amid banks white with mineral salts; the fresh green weeds at the bottom are also refreshing to behold. When heavy showers fall, connection is made with the [Sonoyta] River and the same minnows which were seen there were splashing in the streamlet up to its very sources. The dam, of only moderate size, made a charming impression with the surrounding trees and bushes here and there reflected in it."

Lumholz, who had been drinking brackish water for 20 days before reaching Quitobaquito, reflected: "The little stream of crystal clear spring water at Quitovaquita (sic) is smaller than a brook, but it seemed much alive as it hurried in its effort to keep the dam full. As I had been unaccustomed to seeing running water . . . the tiny brook seemed almost unreal and was enchanting in its effect."

Today, when there is no one else around, there is a quiet, some might say eerie, atmosphere about the place that makes even the wildest stories seem plausible.

One of those wild stories involved a Tohono O'odham girl. Wilton Hoy, a former park ranger at Organ Pipe who has been collecting information about Quitobaquito for more than 20 years, related the story in an unpublished manuscript:

"Arturo Quiroz recalls a near adventure at the pond. One day during a visit to Quitobaquito, Arturo noticed a Papago [Tohono O'odham] girl wearing a large gold ring. Upon inquiring as to the source of the gold, she remained typically silent; however, a query to her father resulted in his atypically instructing his daughter to accompany Arturo to his mine. Arturo drove the girl in a wagon southwest; they were to leave the wagon at Cipriano Ortega's well and walk from there to the mine. As the couple neared the mine, the girl suddenly balked, was obviously frightened, and no amount of persuasion from Arturo could lead her on to the mine, so they returned to Quitobaquito. When they arrived at the pond, the girl's father asked her why she did not continue with Arturo to the mine, and she replied that she had seen a devilish apparition with outstretched claws that warned her if she continued to the mine he would destroy her."

There is no hint today that Quitobaquito once was a fairly active way station. The same can be said of the vast deserts through which El Camino Del Diablo passes. However, on one day in 1989 there was a throng of people assembled at Tule Well, a historic stopping place along the Devil's Highway. The occasion was the 50th anniversary of the establishment of the Cabeza Prieta National Wildlife Refuge. On that day they came, a veritable army of historians, anthropologists, priests, and incurable desert rats.

I saw four men dressed like campesinos suddenly appear. They lifted their rifles and fired toward the setting sun, a warning to the gathering of some 175 spectators below to pay attention: a unique pageant was about to begin. Officials of the wildlife refuge had chosen to celebrate its 50th anniversary with a full-costume dramatization focused on the key figures who crossed this hostile terrain between 1540 and 1900.

The next day Bernard Fontana, at that time field historian for the University of Arizona library, and Bill Broyles sat on a hill looking out over craggy bluffs of the Cabeza Prieta and Gila mountains.

"As each vehicle left," Fontana observed, "it kept getting quieter and quieter, and then — here came the birds, the vultures, the woodpeckers — and within minutes after the last truck left, all the quietness settled in again, and you'd never know that anyone had been there an hour ago."

Six years later I stumbled upon Sestier's grave in the immense and silent desert some 100 miles southeast of Tule Well, and Fontana's words came back to me. But for the cement marker with its small cross above his grave, you'd never know anyone had ever passed that spot before.

(Note: Quitobaquito and other parts of Organ Pipe Cactus National Monument have been closed to the public because of safety concerns. Information is available online at www.nps.gov/orpi/ planyourvisit/yoursafety.htm)

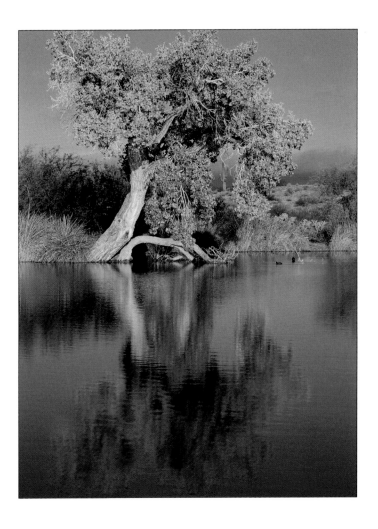

Water tempers the harshness of the Sonoran Desert and forms the basis of tranquil scenes.
(ABOVE) Quitobaquito Spring in Organ Pipe Cactus National Monument has provided a reliable water supply for centuries. JACK DYKINGA

(RIGHT) This man-made pond, named Aguirre's Lake after the man who built it to supply irrigation water, helps nurture life in the Buenos Aires National Wildlife Refuge. Mud flats in the foreground tell the tale of receding water. The remaining pool reflects the majesty of Baboquivari Peak, deemed sacred by the Tohono O'odham Indians. WILLARD CLAY

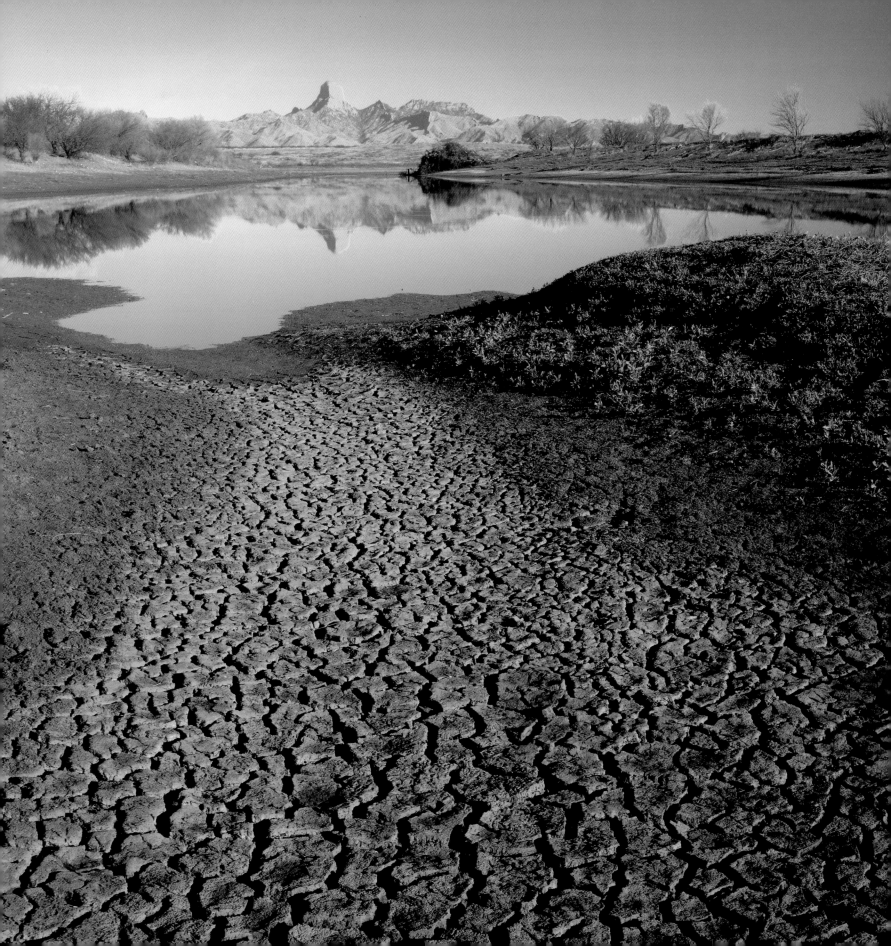

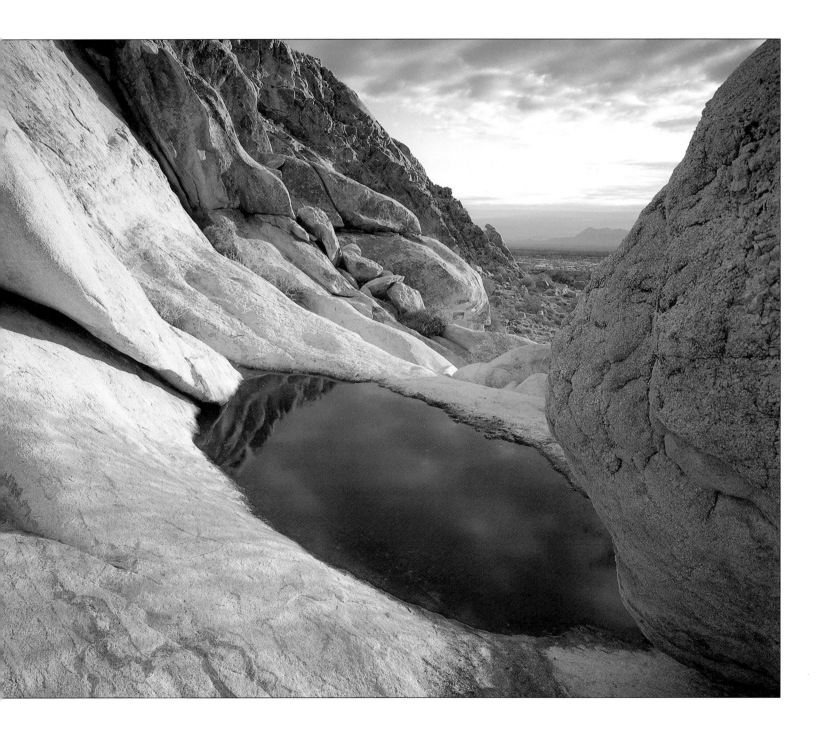

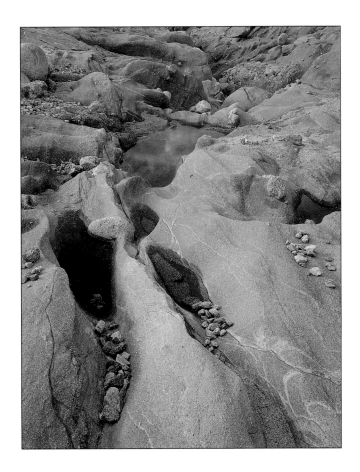

Rocky outcrops in the desert form natural tanks that store precious water left by brief rainstorms. Wildlife depend on these catchments.
(LEFT) Several such tanks are situated in the Tinajas Altas, a mountain range along a route called El Camino del Diablo. GEORGE H.H. HUEY

(ABOVE) These pools are at the base of Baker Peaks, named after a stage coach driver killed in 1871. The peaks' elevation is about 1,400 feet.
WILLARD CLAY

(FOLLOWING PANEL, PAGES 76 AND 77) Hovering over a stock tank, Four Peaks looms as a landmark east of Phoenix in the northern reaches of the desert where cactus blends with scrub brush. Snow from a late spring storm glistens in the setting sun.
JERRY JACKA

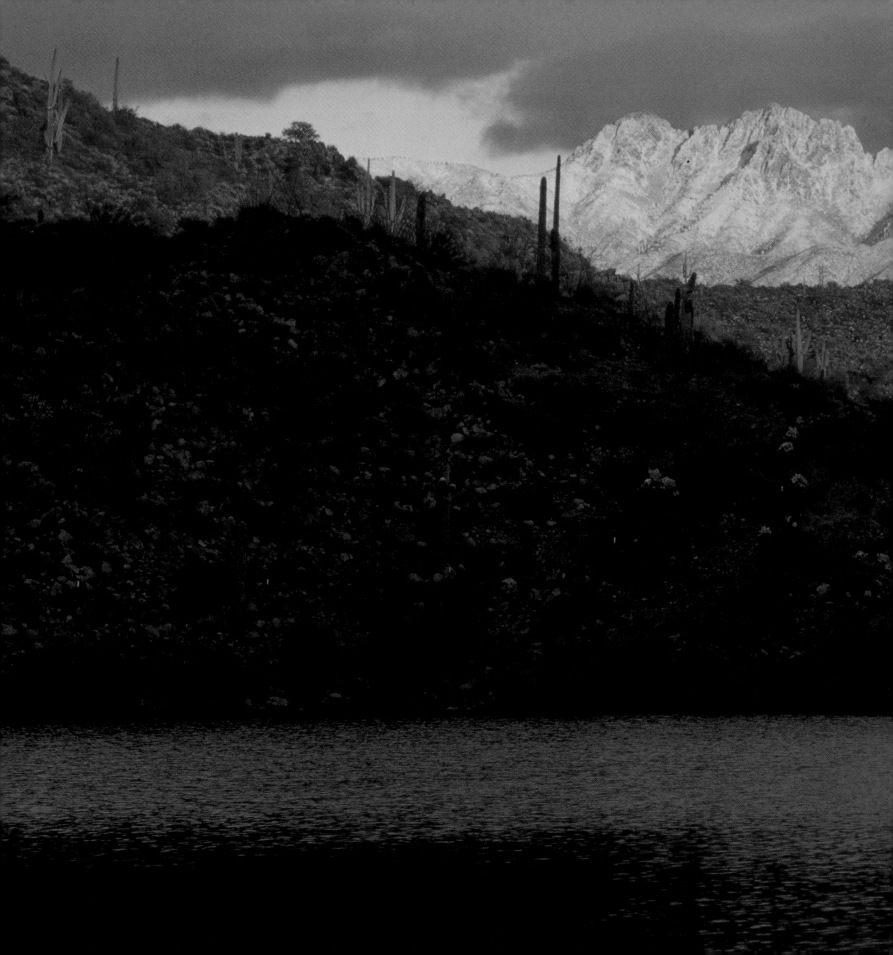

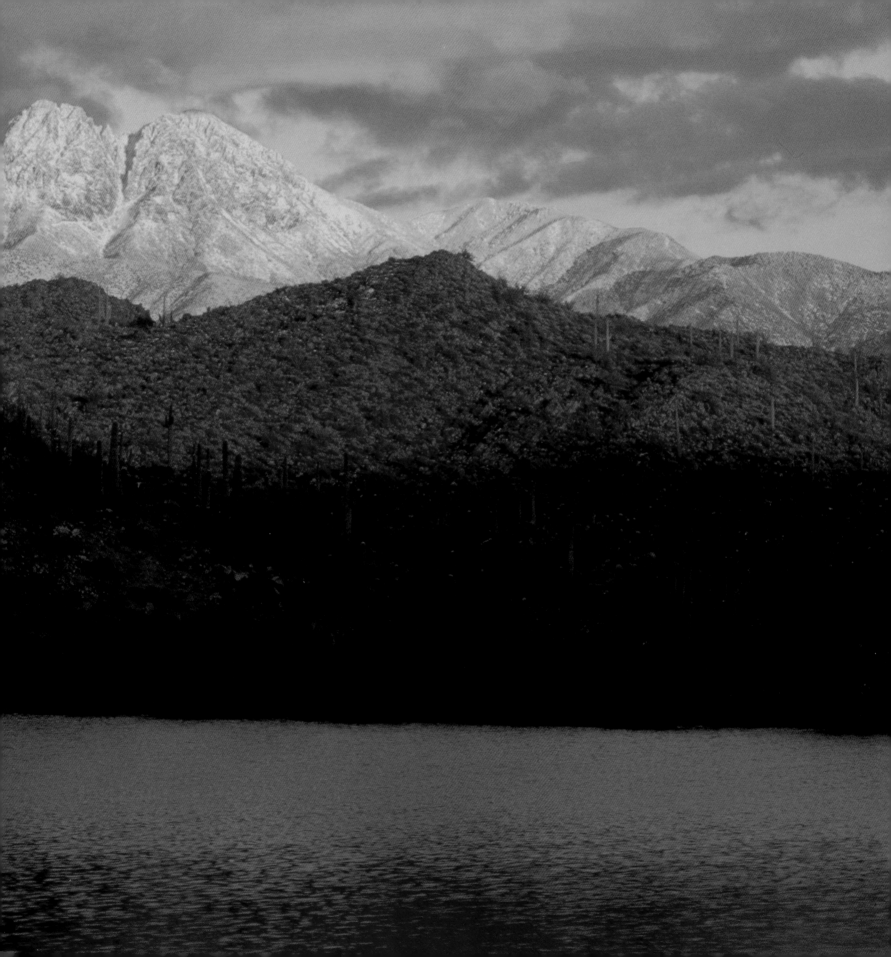

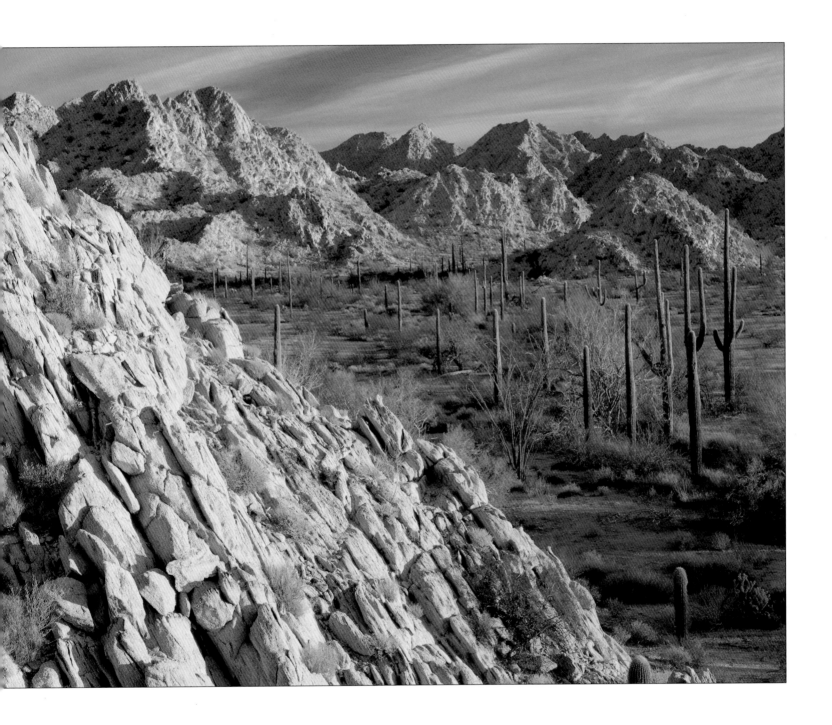

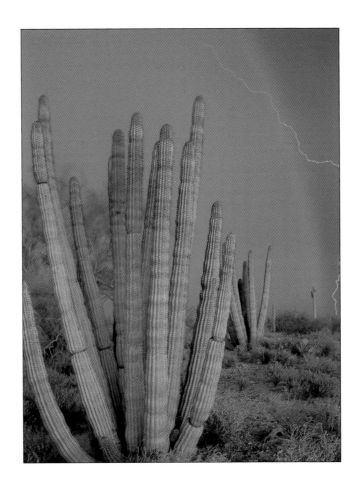

(LEFT) Granite slopes jut from the desert floor in the Cabeza Prieta National Wildlife Refuge, creating a sheltered area for young saguaro cactuses. RANDY PRENTICE

(ABOVE) A storm at sunset bathes organ pipe cactuses in an earthy red haze. The cactus, which blooms in May and June, grows only in southwestern Arizona and northwestern Mexico. The cactus was near extinction in the United States before Organ Pipe Cactus National Monument was established. JACK DYKINGA

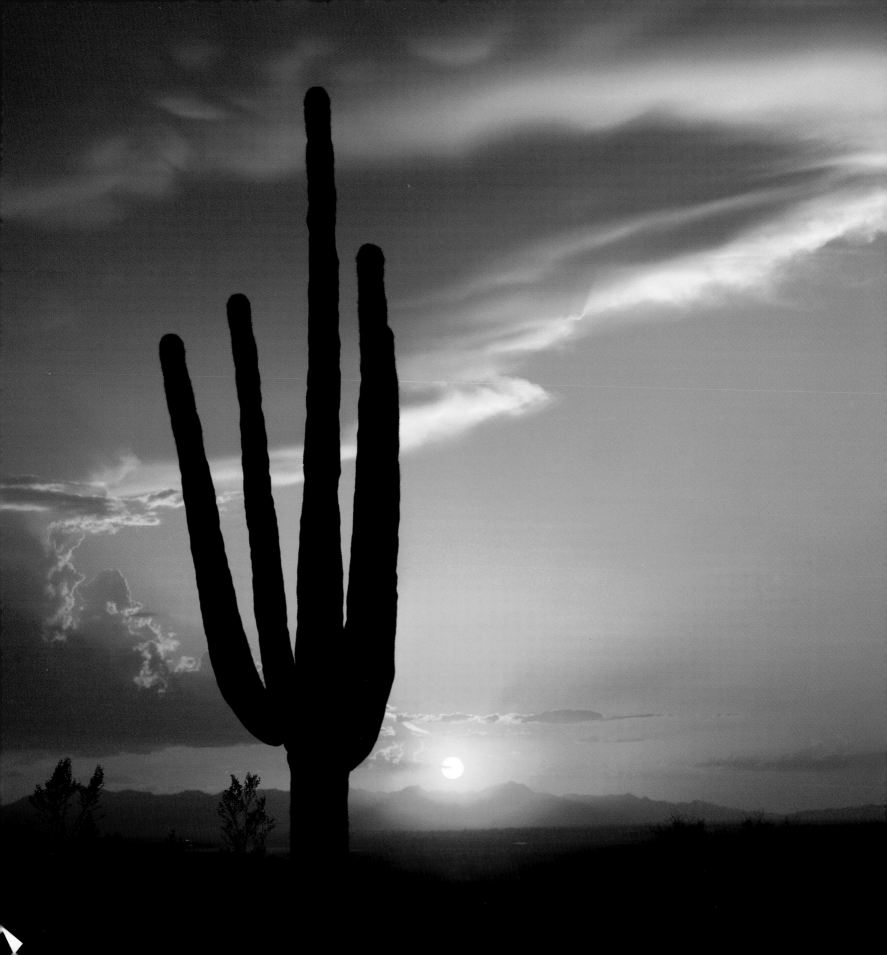

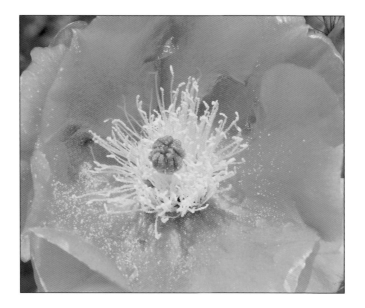

The desert draws brilliant colors from both the sun and vegetation.

(LEFT) Setting behind the Sierra Estrella range west of Phoenix, the sun lavishes the landscape with gold and red hues. BERNADETTE HEATH

(ABOVE) The flower of the prickly pear cactus displays the same hues of gold and red blended together. GEORGE H.H. HUEY

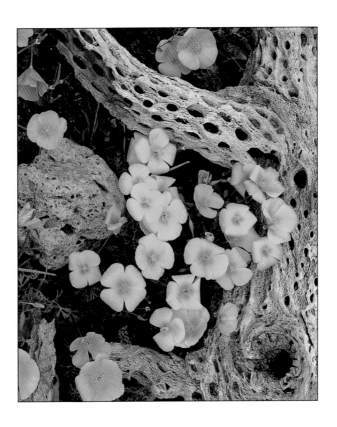

The Mexican goldpoppy is the most popular and most photographed annual wildflower in the desert, often throwing a cloth of gold over slopes, plains, and bajadas (alluvial slopes at the base of a mountain) below 4,000 feet elevation.

(ABOVE) Nestled between a cactus skeleton and a rock in Organ Pipe Cactus National Monument, goldpoppies grow into a natural floral arrangement. WILLARD CLAY

(RIGHT) On a slope beneath a craggy outcrop in the Superstition Mountains east of Phoenix, the poppies are interspersed with blue-violet Coulter's lupine.
TOM DANIELSEN

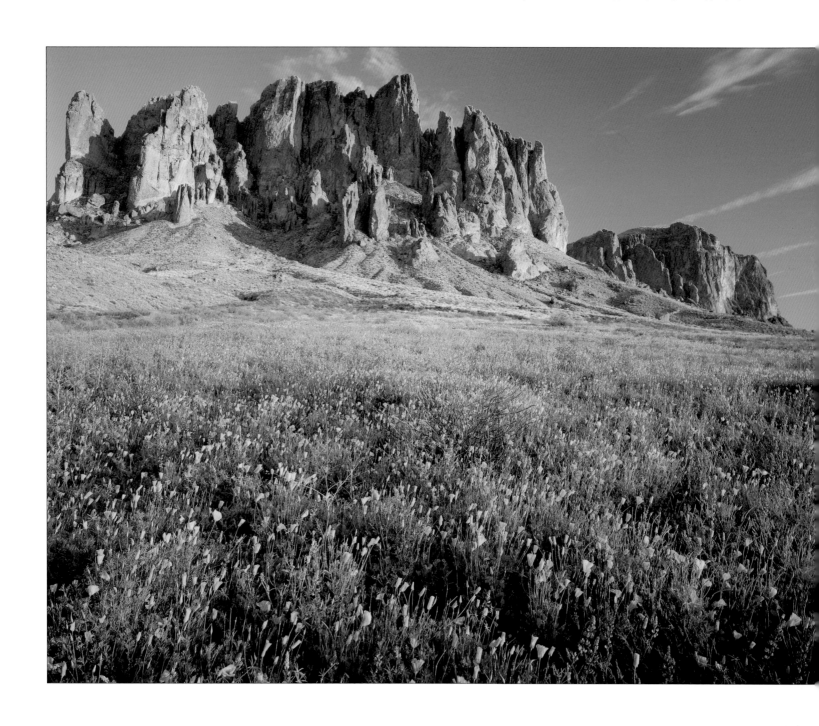

SOUTHEASTERN DESERT

IT IS A PLACE OF DRY RIVERS AND TALL MOUNTAINS. THE SOUTHEASTERN

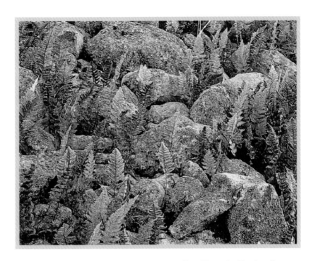

Ferns, rocks, and lichen near the South Fork of Cave Creek in the Chiricahua Mountains form a bouquet in the desert. EDWARD MCCAIN

quarter of Arizona displays a spacious landscape where the vegetation of the Sonoran Desert rolls into the Chihuahuan Desert. It nurtures the giant saguaro cactus and the nearly unbreakable ironwood tree; it provides the habitat needed by creatures as diverse as diminutive elf owls; colorful, tropical birds called elegant trogons; and wild pig-like animals called javelinas. It also fosters a unique version of the legend of La Llorona, a phantom who wanders the dry washes looking for the children she lost in a flash flood.

In 1864 journalist J. Ross Browne left California for an excursion through southern Arizona Territory to write a series of articles for *Harper's Magazine*. When he started he dipped a toe, figuratively speaking, into Arizona at Yuma, and wrote:

"I was now on the borders of a region in which the wildest romance was strangely mingled with the most startling reality. Each day of our sojourn brought with it some fabulous story of discovery or some tragic narrative of suffering and death."

Browne's previous travelogue had dealt with Norway, and he wanted his readers to understand that even though Arizona was significantly different from Scandinavia, it had its own "peculiar charms," and he listed them: "... the absence of accommodation for travelers, and extraordinary advantages in the way of burning deserts, dried rivers, rattlesnakes, scorpions . . . and Apaches."

Browne's account was accurate, as far as it went. But it did not recognize that southeastern Arizona embodies contradictions. Its undulating deserts receive an average of only 12 inches of rain a year, yet amid diminutive trees and shrubs stand pine and spruce-covered mountain ranges often called "sky islands." The contrast is most dramatic in June and July, the hottest months in the desert. In downtown Tucson, the largest city in southern Arizona, it may be 108 degrees, but atop the 9,000-foot high Santa Catalina Mountains, a one-hour drive from the city's center, it likely will be a comfortable 75 or 80 degrees.

Scant as moisture is, there's water enough in some places to sustain springs used by communities. For more than 100 years the tenacious silver mining town of Tombstone has been getting its water from a spring in the Huachuca Mountains, more than 40 miles away.

Southern Arizona is an old place shaped by three cultures whose activities and ambiance are evident in Paleolithic sites, archaeological ruins, remnants of historic buildings, and derivative architectural styles. The area was inhabited first by Indians, later by Spaniards and Mexicans, and more recently by English-speaking settlers.

Scientists say they have proof that the area around the San Pedro River, the only river in southern Arizona that flows year-round, has been inhabited for about 11,200 years. At two points on the river, Murray Springs and a spot now called the Lehner Mammoth Kill Site, archaeologists uncovered the bones of extinct mammoths, camels, and bison that had been killed by people referred to as Clovis Man. There are only 10 known Clovis Man sites in all of North America, and two of them are on the San Pedro River.

The Ice Age landscape where Clovis Man roamed gradually gave way to a drier climate and different cultures. Thousands of years after Clovis Man disappeared, what now is called the Cochise Culture appeared in the area. Archaeologists found remains of these prehistoric people in present-day Cochise County. As the historian Jay J. Wagoner has pointed out, these ancient hunters and root-eaters were a link between the earliest mammoth hunters and later Indians. More recently, the land once populated by Clovis Man, the Cochise Culture, and the Hohokam Indians, belonged to Spain.

Friar Marcos de Niza was the first to intentionally explore Arizona for Spain in 1539 during a trek from Culiacan, Mexico, to the vicinity of what is now Zuni, New Mexico, and he may have followed the San Pedro River through southern Arizona for part of his journey. In 1938 another priest, the late Bonaventure Oblasser, translated de Niza's vague report on his journey and decided he had camped along the river near Fairbank on April 14, 1539. But the truth is that no one knows for sure what route de Niza took because his notes were imprecise.

A year after de Niza was in the area, the explorer Francisco Vasquez de Coronado, whose journey was well-documented, trekked into what is now Arizona near

Palominas and for a time followed a river the Indians called Nexpa (now called the San Pedro). In 1692 the explorer-missionary Eusebio Kino came to southern Arizona looking for converts and sites to establish missions. Some of these missions still exist, and one — San Xavier del Bac in Tucson — serves a primarily Tohono O'odham Indian congregation.

One of the most evocative historical sites in southern Arizona is the 200-year-old adobe ruin of the Spanish presidio (or fort) that was known as Santa Cruz de Terrenate. The Terrenate ruins at Fairbank have been thoroughly studied by archaeologist Jack Williams, who observed during a visit a few years ago:

"This was not a fun place to be in 1776. The Spaniards came here as conquerors and left as evacuees. I have a feeling there were a lot of deserters from this place, because it seems you had a choice of dying here or someplace else."

Williams' wry comment about mortality was not flippant; he based it on reports written 200 years ago by Teodoro de Croix, commander of the Northern Frontier of New Spain. Those documents indicate that assignment to Santa Cruz de Terrenate was like a wave goodbye. The presidio was used from 1775 to 1780, and Williams noted that there never were more than 60 men stationed there at one time, yet 80 men were killed there.

"In addition to heavy casualties," Williams said, "the presidio commander at Santa Cruz de Terrenate continued to face the problem of having only partially completed facilities to house and protect his men. Furthermore, the repeated attacks of the Apaches prevented the harvesting of the crops. . . . As a result, soldiers and settlers at the fort were literally starving to death."

Grim and dangerous as that era in southern Arizona was, it provided nothing to match the bizarreness of a skirmish that occurred 66 years later at a point on the San Pedro River called Charleston Crossing, just 10 miles south of the abandoned presidio. The incident in 1846 has come to be known as "The Battle of the Bulls."

There is a plaque on a boulder near the spot where Lt. Col. Philip St. George Cooke and his 500 soldiers of "The Mormon Battalion" were attacked, not by Indians, but by wild bulls. The U.S. Army had assigned Cooke and his men — known as the Mormon Battalion because all were members of the Church of Jesus Christ of Latter-day Saints — to open a wagon road from Santa Fe, New Mexico, to San Diego, California. Odie B. Faulk, an Arizona historian, described what happened when Cooke and his men innocently spooked a bunch of bulls lying in the shade of some honey mesquites:

". . . the battalion was attacked by wild, ferocious bulls. A private was tossed in the air and gored in the leg. The same bull eviscerated a mule before being felled by rifle fire. Col. Cooke, when confronted by an enormous bull, prepared to make a run for his life. Luckily, a corporal shot the animal, and it died practically at Cooke's feet. Lt. George Stoneman almost shot off his own thumb while trying to kill a bull. Cooke in his journal referred to this incident as 'The Battle of

Bull Run,' anticipating the Civil War battle by some fifteen years."

Southeastern Arizona has attracted miners since the Spaniards in the 16th century. During the late 19th century, silver strikes in Tombstone initiated development of sites where ore was smelted and loaded on trains. You can still see remains of such places as Charleston, once called Millville, and Contention City.

The picture changed drastically in 1887 when an earthquake shocked the San Pedro Valley, destroying the mill towns, flooding the silver mines, and igniting a fire that decimated most of the grasses, willows, and cottonwoods in the basin.

It took nearly 100 years for the vegetation to return to normal. Today thick stands of cottonwoods, ablaze in yellow and orange foliage in the fall, help define the Sonoita Creek Sanctuary in Patagonia, one of several wildlife viewing areas owned by The Nature Conservancy and open to the public. Another Nature Conservancy site, the pine-oak forest of Ramsey Canyon in the Huachuca Mountains

near Sierra Vista, is known as "The Hummingbird Capital of the World" because more than 14 species of the bird have been spotted there.

Bisbee, once dubbed the Queen of the Copper Camps, now uses its mining past as a foundation for a tourist industry. A picturesque town built on terraces rising from a gulch in the Mule Mountains, Bisbee is host each October to a unique stair-climbing race called "The Bisbee 1,000." Participants run up nine staircases, former burro paths, and 1,034 steps.

While Bisbee attracts increasing numbers, it still hasn't matched Tombstone's draw, which centers on the gunfight at the O.K. Corral. The steely-eyed Wyatt Earp was Tombstone's most famous lawman and the central figure in the gunfight, which became Hollywood's most famous metaphor for the triumph of good over evil in the Wild West. At least once a month, local performers re-enact the gunfight on the spot where it occurred in 1881.

Tombstone preserves other attractions, among them the Bird Cage Theater,

which the *New York Times* referred to in 1882 as the wildest and most wicked night spot between Basin Street and the Barbary Coast. Now a museum, the place was named for the 14 cages suspended from the ceiling over the dance hall and gambling casino. The cages were display cases for prostitutes.

Tombstone, like much of southeastern Arizona, was a place populated by "gamblers, horse thieves, murderers, and vagrant politicians," which was J. Ross Browne's blanket assessment of all of southern Arizona. Browne made his trip before Tombstone was founded, yet he still concluded that southern Arizona was "a paradise of devils."

Never did he anticipate that birds, trees, and a few quaint buildings in a defunct mining town would convert the unsavory outposts he visited to alluring destinations for visitors and settlers looking for an agreeable place to live.

88

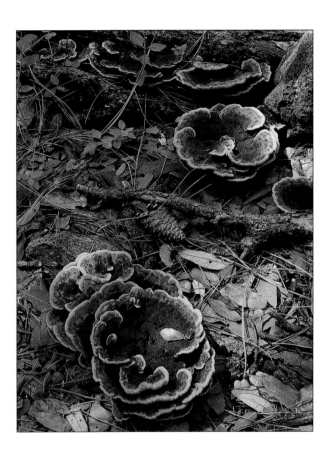

(ABOVE) An appealing still life of fungi, oak leaves, and pine cones decorates the forest floor, reflecting the botanical diversity of the mountains that rise abruptly from southeastern Arizona's desert valleys.
JACK DYKINGA

(RIGHT) Autumn leaves swirl in the waters of the South Fork of Cave Creek in the Chiricahua Mountains.
RANDY PRENTICE

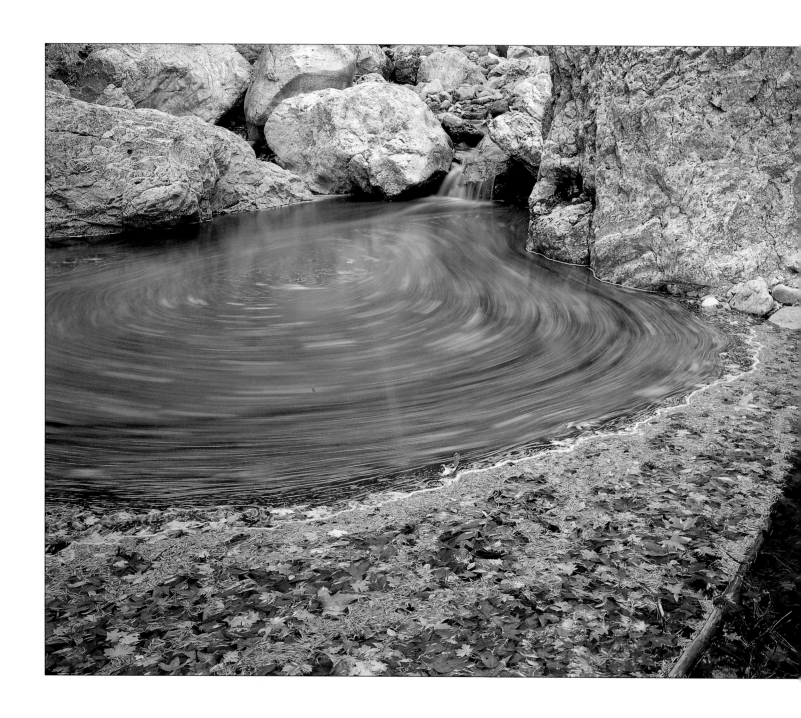

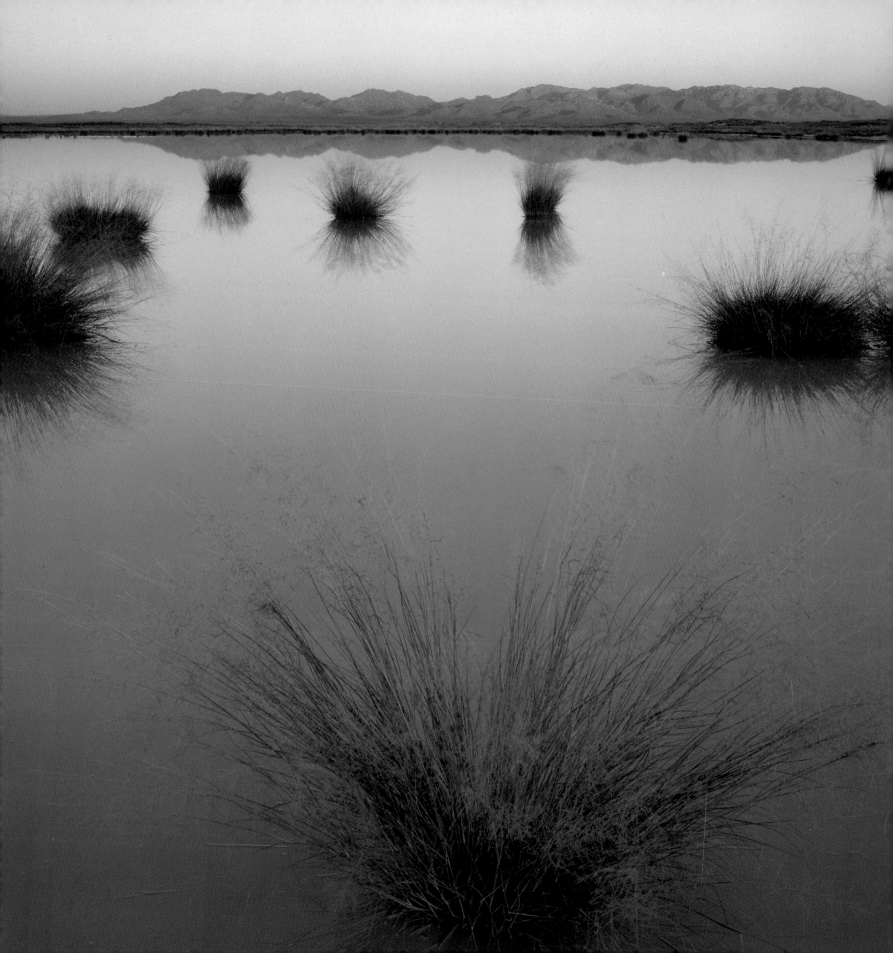

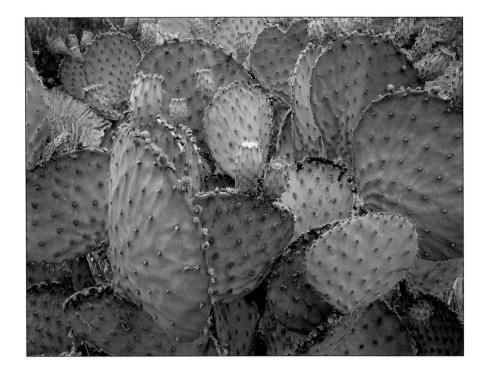

(LEFT) Tufts of grass sprout from the shallow waters of Willcox Playa. Dry most of the year, each winter the playa (Spanish for "beach") fills with rain water and becomes home for more than 12,000 migrating sandhill cranes. The large, gray birds have a seven-foot wingspan and a haunting bugling cry. JACK DYKINGA

(ABOVE) Purple prickly pear cactuses grow in elevations between 2,000 and 5,000 feet in the Sonoran and Chihuahuan deserts of southeastern Arizona, producing brilliant yellow flowers in April and May. RANDY PRENTICE

(FOLLOWING PANEL, PAGES 92 AND 93) Finger Rock in the Santa Catalina Mountains north of Tucson snags a cloud left behind by a clearing storm. RANDY PRENTICE

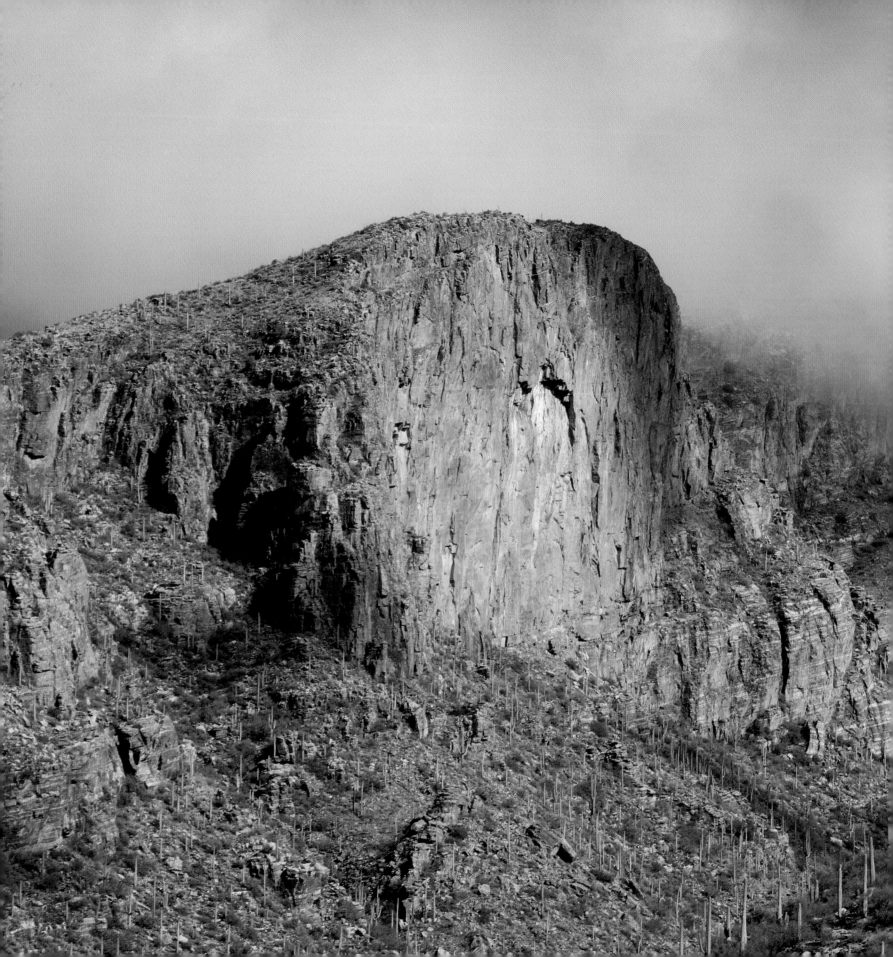

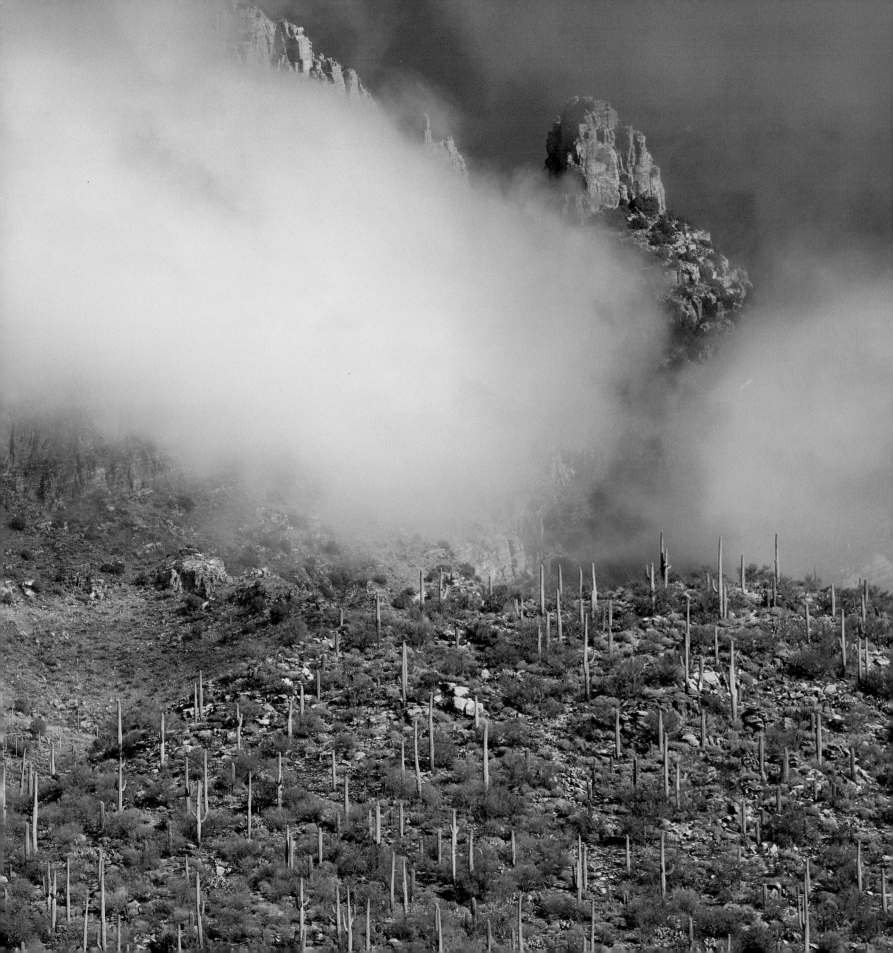

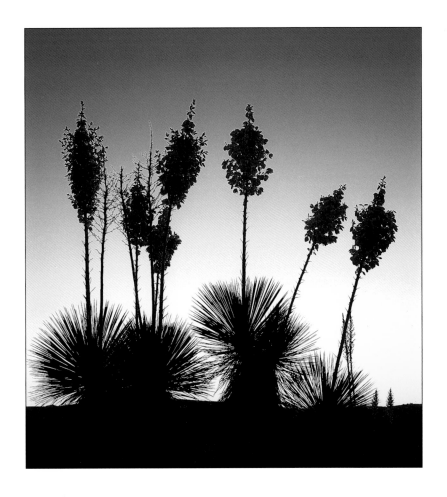

(LEFT) Sunrise illuminates the ridgelines of the Chiricahua Mountains, the ancestral home of the Chiricahua Apaches. For four centuries these fierce warriors swept down from their mountain stronghold to raid other Indians and Spanish and Anglo interlopers in southeastern Arizona. DAVID MUENCH

(ABOVE) Sunset silhouettes yuccas in the full bloom of early summer. The yucca and a desert moth enjoy a symbiotic relationship that both rely on for survival. The moth pollinates the yucca flower by pushing pollen into the tube of the flower's stigma, then lays its eggs in the yucca fruit, which will provide food for the moth larvae upon hatching. BRUCE GRIFFIN (FOLLOWING PAGE) Sunset ignites the storm clouds over the saguaro forest in Sabino Canyon northeast of Tucson. DAVID W. LAZAROFF

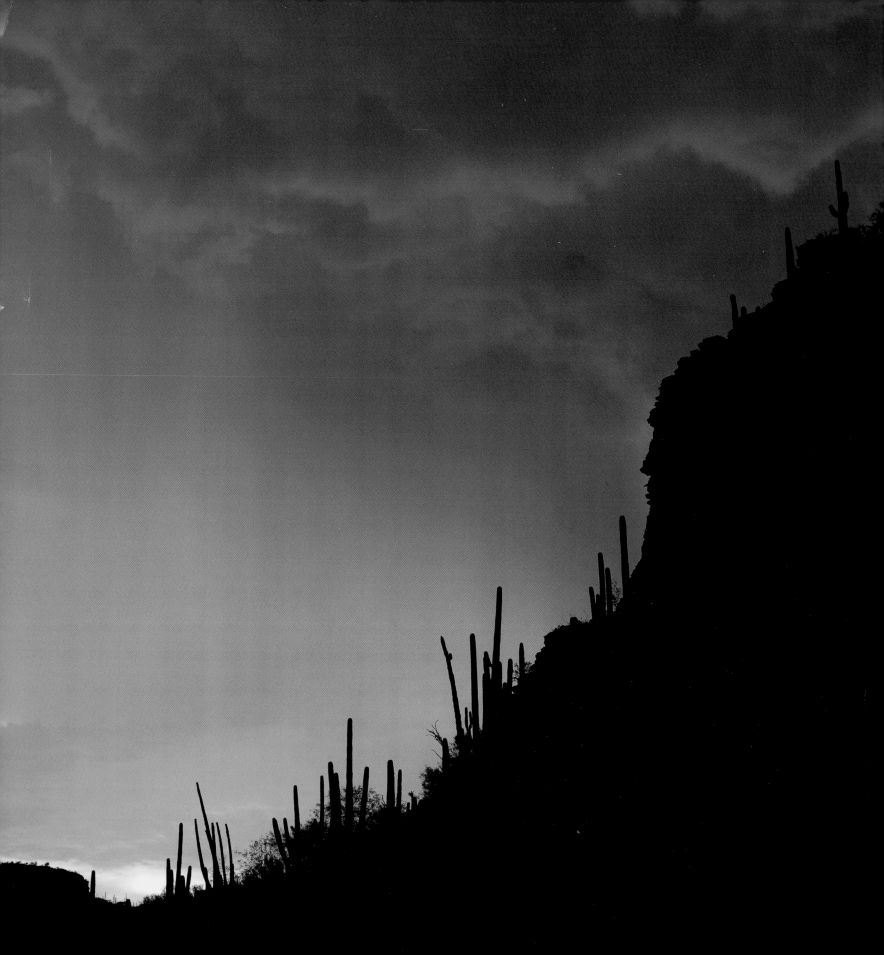